bush
PUBLISHING
& associates

ENDORSEMENTS

When my children were in junior high school, I told them I wanted them to meet a joyful Christian. I took them to meet this man! Buy his book, and share in the joy of the Lord with Rod Kendrick.

–Rev Eddie Brown, PhD

Stumps is excellent! This man has overcome every obstacle imaginable and he Triumphs through life.
I am so blessed to know him.

–CMA Preacher Dennis Matlock

I've known Rodney for more than 20 years. We served together in the ministry of the Christian Motorcyclists Association. Together we went places where most are scared to go. We built relationships and shared Christ with some of the hardest of the hardcore motorcyclists. Together we saw God do amazing things.

During all of this Rodney was as enthusiastic, and worked as hard, if nor harder, than everyone else. His lack of legs didn't hold him back. He was always happy, upbeat, and encouraged others whose problems were really minor compared to his own. I can honestly say Rodney was (is) an inspiration to me. **–Kerry Gibson, Master, US Merchant Marine (Ret) & National Vice President Christian Motorcyclists Association (Ret)**

MY THOUSAND POUND GORILLA

My Thousand Pound Disability Becomes
A Thousand Possibilities

Written by
Rod (Stumps) Kendrick

bush
PUBLISHING
& associates

Unless otherwise indicated, all Scripture quotations are taken from the New King James Version of the Bible, copyright © 1979, 1980, 1982, Thomas Nelson, Inc., Publishers.
All Scripture quotations marked KJV are taken from the King James Version of the Bible.

MY THOUSAND POUND GORILLA
ISBN: 978-1-944566-37-1
ISBN: 978-1-944566-38-8
Copyright © 2023 by Bush Publishing & Associates
Bush Publishing & Associates, LLC books may be ordered at everywhere and at Amazon.com

For further information, please contact:
Bush Publishing & Associates
Tulsa, Oklahoma
www.bushpublishing.com

Printed in the United States of America.

No portion of this book may be used or reproduced by any means: graphic, electronic or mechanical, including photocopying, recording, taping, or by any information storage retrieval system, without the written permission of the publisher, except in the case of brief quotations embodied in critical articles and reviews.

DEDICATION

I dedicate this book to Vienna, my wife, ghost-writer, editor, helpmate, my destiny, companion & friend. Without her, this book could not have been completed.

ACKNOWLEDGEMENTS

I must first give thanks to I AM, Lord God Jehovah, Yahweh for creating me in the womb.

To the King of Glory Jesus Christ who loves me, a sinner saved by Grace.

To my wife and ghost-writer, Vienna Schuering.

To Bonnie Litterell for overall editing and story flow.

To Barbara Lassiter for the perfect stone altar illustration.

To all of my family and friends that walked with me on this journey.

FOREWORD

I met Rod Kendrick about ten years ago when he wheeled up to me at a Celebrate Recovery meeting. I had just given my testimony and he wanted to thank me and shake my hand. He was congenial and we struck up a casual conversation. After that we often sat together for dinner before our large CR group met.

Over the months, I came to know and respect him. He was a double amputee in a wheelchair, but there was not a drop of self-pity in him. One way or another, he could get anywhere he wanted to go. He was a man of God whose "yes" was "yes" and whose "no" was "no". He never pretended to be faultless. On the contrary, he quietly owned his past, the good. the bad and the sometimes downright ugly. He was funny and self-deprecating. The women in CR all liked him and without exception, the men respected him. He talked about the healing power of Jesus Christ even as he sat in a wheelchair. He did not see how powerful his own testimony was.

A year later he asked me for a date. It was a motorcycle fundraiser for a brother-in-Christ who had been shot. I was fascinated with how he rolled his chair onto his specially built sidecar, tied it down and sidled over to the seat on his Harley-Davidson Sportster. Rod seat-buckled me into his wheelchair and I rode on the platform all day. The riding setup was probably illegal, but we never got stopped. By the time we finished the day, I was totally disarmed by his charm and laughter.

We dated for a year and a half and then abruptly broke it off. The truth is we were both still damaged from our past bad choices and even now were not doing things God's way. For the next year and a half, we hardly spoke. Rod will share how God brought us back together later in his book. He loves to tell that story. Even though it makes me cringe, I wouldn't rob him of the pleasure of telling it. We were married May 28, 2017.

The longer I know Rod, the more I like and respect him. He introduces me to everyone as his "Proverbs 31 Wife". We understand each other. We share every hope and dream. We laugh. We can talk about God, money and politics without a single raised eyebrow because we walk in agreement. We are evenly yoked, something neither of us knew anything about. We both love and understand the other's inner child. He shares the Word of God everyday with me. He prays with me and for me. I have never known a better man than Rod Kendrick. In the words of Rascal Flatts, "God blessed the broken road that led me straight to you."

Rod and I have a lot in common. We have both married multiple times and made terrible decisions. We have both overcome our pasts and together we have built a marriage full of hope, promise and peace. Rod's upbringing and early childhood experiences scarred him, but his honesty and faith in God have healed him. He is a source of encouragement and strong faith that touches everyone around him.

Rod is a "rolling" testimony of the healing power and grace of Jesus Christ. It doesn't matter where you start out, how many bad decisions you have made, God can and will use you when you put your trust in Him. Rod's story will encourage you and give you hope, no matter how many times you have done it wrong.

Vienna Schuering

Rod's Happy Wife

TABLE OF CONTENTS

Endorsements iii
Dedication vii
Acknowledgements viii
Foreword xi
1: Oblivion 1
2: Painful Beginnings 3
3: The Hidden Secret 14
4: Culture Shock, Pot, And Jesus 26
5: The Running Years 37
6: Working 49
7: Hurt, Doubt And Confusion 55
8: The Bicycle Ride 67
9: And Finally, God 78
10: Thriving, But Challenged 87
11: My Seven Year Dream 101
12: Make A Dollar, Spend Three 118
13: The Quiet After The Storm 128
14: Healing And Grace 137
15: My Memorial Stone Altar 148

1

Oblivion

September 3, 1981 was a Thursday and my life changed forever. I was 27, wild and free, flying down the highway in my 1980 Z-28 Camaro. I was on the way to see my girl and the possibilities of the night were expectantly before me.

The weather was clear and hot. The drive was scenic and green on the two-lane curvy Highway 43 between New Hebron and Purvis, MS. My foot was heavy on the accelerator, but my mood was light as I daydreamed about how good my life was.

Life was way better than good. I was fit and jogged five miles every day. I was a bachelor with a degree in outdoor recreation and resources management. I had a well-paying career that kept me outdoors. I had a quick smile and easy wit. I loved the ladies and the ladies loved me.

I would never have admitted that I was running from God, running scared for all I was worth. Partying and drinking did not bring me peace, but more turmoil. I was angry to my bones over things from my youth that had never been addressed. No amount of praying, drinking or chasing women brought me peace. I was having a lot of fun, but there was no peace. No joy. No contentment. In fact, I was about to enter my own personal hell and only God could pull me out.

My mind drifted back to my plans for the evening. I was taking my girl out to eat and for a whirl around the dance floor. It didn't matter that I had put in a full day and was physically exhausted, I could handle it. But, no, I drifted off in spite of myself. My Camaro veered off the road, crashed through a barbed-wire fence and was cut in half by a mature pine tree close to the road. My car was demolished and I was thrown into the back seat, legs crushed and bleeding. I knew nothing for the next six weeks.

2

Painful Beginnings

My early years are filled with fear, yelling, trying to hide, and blank spots where I can't remember anything. My dad was an angry man, subject to fits of rage and screaming. His attitude was often "hit it, kick it, break it, cuss it." My mother was not exempt from these rages and my father beat my mother. They both drank too much. While Dad's rages did not include hitting my sisters or me, his behavior was terrifying. Just because he didn't hit us, didn't mean he wouldn't.

One of my earliest memories is of Dad taking me fishing when I was only four or five. He had found a small pond close to a drive-in theater not far from home. We had cane poles and a five-gallon bucket half full of crawdads for bait. I was excited about catching a fish, but I was afraid of those crawdads.

My dad said, "Hey, son, reach in and grab a crawdad." I looked down in that bucket and all I could see were thousands of sharp red pinchers. I froze in fear as Dad continued to yell, "Reach in and get one! Reach in and get one!" The more he yelled, the more afraid I became and backed away from the bucket.

The next thing I knew, I was flat on my back screaming in terror. He had me pinned down under his knees, he was astride my chest pouring the bucket of crawdads all over my face and chest. His face was contorted in rage as he screamed "They don't bite! They don't bite!" Horrified, I screamed and choked on the water and tried to wiggle away but couldn't. Eventually, he came to his senses and got off me. He removed the crawdads that were hanging on my clothes and stood me up. He did not apologize, he said not a word as he silently loaded me in the car and took me home. I never said a word to my mother, but my future relationship with my father was set in stone that day. I could not stand up to him and I would be forever terrified of him and his unpredictable rages.

My father and I would have several fishing disasters, and frankly, I don't know why he continued to take me. They always ended in a nightmare of one kind or another. Dad, Mom, and I went fishing in a small pond with a white sandy bottom, and crystal water, and once again, crawdads were clearly visible. I was wearing shorts, a pullover, and flip-flops.

Carefully, I entered the water to follow tiny fish while trying to avoid those scary-biting crawfish. Only knee-deep into the pond, I screamed with terror when something touched the back of my right leg. I remember my dad roaring with laughter and my mother snatching me out of the water. The culprit that had scared me was one of my own flip-flops that had come off and touched me on the leg. Mother snuggled with me and gave me comfort, Dad continued to laugh and I began to hate.

I had three sisters, Michelle Renee, Dawn Richelle, and Shawn Raylene. Mom endearingly called us the four "R's." Living with them meant that I lost out on all votes. Whatever it was that they wanted to do is what we did. One of their favorite things to do was go to the pond and feed the ducks and their babies. I was not the least bit interested in feeding the ducks, I wanted to go ride my minibike, but they delighted in those fuzzy little babies.

All three girls were sun-bleached blondes who tanned like little brown biscuits in the California sun. They got along and played like any other little girls. There were often giggles and there was very little squabbling. All four of us were afraid of the wrath of DAD, (who we called WG when he wasn't around). Dad liked to have a beer, lie down on the living room floor, and watch TV. He always fell asleep. We learned to steer clear of him while he slept and none of us dared to change the TV channel. If we woke him up, there would be hell to pay.

We always had a horse so most of our activities were outside the house. Our first horse, Pinta, was a sorrel with a white star on her forehead. She was an old nag and quite gentle. Pinta belonged to the girls, but I was allowed to ride her. One day while riding bareback Pinta jumped a small dry creek bed, I fell off her. I landed hard directly under her foot. The instant Pinta felt my chest under her hoof, she lifted it. I was shaken, but unharmed. She was a perfect horse for all of us and I rode her often.

The girls had their chores and I had mine. I did the usual boy things like take out the trash and mow the grass. Beginning in about sixth grade, I dragged brush for my father's business and helped load it on the truck. This is a job that continued until I moved off to attend college. WG didn't pay me in cash, but in other ways. He bought me a motorized mini-bike and when I was older, he bought me cars and gave me gas money, dating money and eventually, he paid all of my college expenses.

One day Mom was visiting neighbors and WG thought she had been gone too long. He took my minibike to go hunt for her. Somewhere along the way, he crashed my bike with the 3 HP Briggs and Stratton engine on a blue frame, with a black seat and chrome ape hanger handlebars. It was my pride and joy. It was a Christmas present one year, so in reality, WG paid for it and in his own mind, it was his to ride whenever he wanted. Later WG came stomping into the house with a black eye and road rash on his face and arms. I thought that black eye was justice dished up to the one who deserved it.

I was often the unpaid babysitter for my sisters. I wasn't that old and responsible, but I was good enough to watch the three of them for short periods of time. Our house was in Vista, high on a ridgeline thick with vegetation. Fire danger is a yearly threat in Southern California, and one afternoon while watching the girls the smell of smoke drifted through the house. When I looked outside, I could see huge clouds of smoke in the air and even see the flames of the fire. Panic set in. I was alone with the girls and the fire was advancing toward our house.

Something inside of me screamed, "Get out now!" I grabbed my little red wagon and started rounding up my terrified sisters. One by one, I plunked each of them in the wagon. I threw a blanket over them to keep the smoke out. I had to get them out and to safety, but I wasn't sure where to go. I pulled the wagon out into the street and two fire trucks with sirens blaring flew past us racing toward the oncoming fire. My sisters were wailing in fear and I was pulling that wagon as hard as I could to get them to safety. They were heavy and it was all I could do to lean forward and heave them away from the fire.

As we trudged up the block, I could see Florence and Carl's house. They didn't live very far from us, only a few houses. They were nice old German neighbors and I headed toward their house hoping they were home and could help. I huffed and puffed up their driveway with my crying sisters in tow and stopped at their front door. I pounded on their door crying out for help. The door was thrown open and the shocked faces of Florence and Carl appeared. They grabbed us up and welcomed us into their house. We had cookies and Kool-Aid while the fire department contained the fire. I was the big brother hero for saving my sisters. Eventually, our parents came home and retrieved us. Our house wasn't damaged and things quickly settled back to normal.

Up until this time we lived in a very small house. My three sisters had one bedroom and Mom and Dad had the other. I slept on the couch. It was cramped and I was glad when we moved to a different house. There was a lot more room and I had my own bedroom, which suited me just fine and there was room for a horse and plenty of area to play.

I also had a fair amount of freedom. In the summertime, I was allowed to fix my own breakfast. Peanut butter on toast was my favorite. All it took was a paper towel and a knife and no mess left behind in Mom's spotless kitchen. Out the door, I ran. I'd hop on my bike and fly down the drive. The whole day was before me. Dusk and curfew were light-years away. I made a lot of friends and we buddied the summers away. We each had something to contribute and those days were fun and memorable.

Ernie lived across the street. His family had a pool and there was always an open invitation to swim. The pool was enclosed behind a big wooden privacy fence, but I had entrance to the pool. We'd splash and swim around and do stupid stuff as young boys do. We spent hours together wasting the day in the warm sunshine endlessly playing Marco Polo. Sometimes his sister and her friend would join us and we'd splash water on them and annoy them until they got mad and left. We howled at our success in running them off and having the pool to ourselves.

My friend Allen had a snooker table in his garage and he lived right down the street. His father had taught him how to play, so Allen taught us. Ernie would come over and a couple of other guys and we'd play snooker until darkness forced us to go home. We weren't great players; we were just barely tall enough to reach the table. Allen was the best player so he always won no matter how hard we tried to beat him. We'd play game after game every night. Then, we'd come back the next day and do it all over again.

Michael was a great friend and the smartest boy in my class. He always had the correct answer to any question the teacher asked. Michael had no brothers, only an older sister. We became like brothers holding our own against all the girls in our lives. Michael lived a mile or so away, but on my bike, the distance was quickly covered. I didn't have to be home until dark and we made the most of our time. We did all kinds of interesting science experiments out in the garage. He would load up a beaker of chemicals and I was thrilled when foam spewed out or bubbled over. We wore no eye protection, who knew what was in the chemicals we inhaled. Protective gloves did not exist outside of moms who did dishes in the kitchen. We didn't care about safety, we didn't even know what safety was. We only knew we were doing important science "stuff." I never missed a chance to go over to Michael's and do science experiments.

The guys all came to my house to run wild on the land. Pinta was there to make things interesting. We could ride her or not, and most of the time we ignored her. We often sprawled in the grass and looked at the clear blue sky. Sometimes we talked, sometimes we didn't. My friends would come over whenever WG wasn't home because we were all afraid of him.

Dad and I had one more memorable fishing adventure. In southern California, dairy farming is big business and there was a large Borden Dairy close to our house. This dairy had an inviting pond with cattails growing here and there around it. The lush, grassy land was surrounded by a barbed-wire fence. There were no signs hung that said to keep out, so we crawled through the fence carrying our can of worms and fishing poles. We were two illegal anglers on the bank of that pond. It was just after sunrise and we hoped to get lucky and catch a fish or two. I was daydreaming and watching my bobber when Dad suddenly yelled "Run!"

Startled, I looked up to see a rider on horseback galloping straight at us. He was wearing a big sombrero and carrying a lever-action rifle that he was waving in the air while he yelled "Get out of here! Get out of here!"

We scrambled to our feet and ran like Satan himself was after us. I was the farthest away from the rider, so I led the charge to escape. There was a heavy thicket of bushes about 25 yards away and I headed for them. Blindly, I dove into the thickest area and froze. Dad piled on behind me in short order. Both of us lay there gasping for breath while trying to be silent.

The rider came pounding up close to the thicket searching for us. His horse was winded, gasping for air and snorting loud enough to cover our own gasps for air. I could plainly see the horseman's clean-shaven angry face. Several times he circled the thicket looking for us before he gave up and turned his horse's head in another direction.

After some time, we quietly snuck out, fishing rods in hand, but no fish. I was furious because we could have been arrested or shot or who knows what. Never, not one time, did I feel that Dad ever watched out for me. With Dad, it was always 'every man for himself.' This could have been a funny cautionary tale that Dad and I would share and laugh about in the future. I never felt safe enough with Dad to laugh about anything.

At some point, my father was diagnosed as manic-depressive, (bi-polar in today's language). He refused to take medication and drank excessive amounts of alcohol. He was scary, loud, angry beyond description, and controlled everything around him, except for himself. His word was law and there was no escaping his wrath. We did not talk about Dad's anger, his mental health issues, or his drinking. How we lived was our secret and I thought it was normal until I saw how my buddies lived. Their dads were fun and caring and there was never any yelling or screaming when I was there.

One Sunday morning when my sisters and I were sitting at the dining room table. The food was hot and the aroma of French toast and bacon was mouthwatering. We fidgeted in anticipation as we waited for Dad to join us. Dad was outside and I could hear his loud, angry cursing as he threw open the front door and exploded into the dining room. As he stomped past the table, he swiped it clean in one sweeping motion. Plates crashed and the silverware clanged. Glasses of orange juice, plates of French toast, eggs, and bacon all crashed to the floor in a broken, sticky mess covered in maple syrup. Paper napkins fluttered over the mess. We sat in stunned silence at the table as Dad stalked into the kitchen. There Dad raged at Mom and an angry exchange of words followed. There was no hitting this time and the storm passed when Dad charged out of the house. He was gone for hours.

Mom came out of the kitchen and silently started to clean up the mess. Her face was set, but there were no tears. All of us scrambled to help her and together we cleaned up the mess. We had cereal for breakfast that day.

This was the everyday environment in the Kendrick household. Dad's explosive fits of anger, his unprovoked rages, and his breaking things were how we lived. This was my example growing up, and just because I was too scared to blow up at Dad, didn't mean I wasn't just as angry as he was. I felt so helpless and so angry and there was nothing I could do to stop him. Our home was a battlefield and surviving the war at home was how all of us lived.

Mom and Dad both drank, sometimes to excess. One night when they had a date Grandpa Pepe came home instead of our parents. The story came to us in fuzzy pieces over time and this is what I put together. They were at a bar drinking and a man made a pass at Mom. Dad thought she responded with a smile and a wink. Dad beat the hell out of Mom then and there at the bar in front of everyone. He pounded her face until she was black, blue, and bleeding and had to be taken to the hospital. Grandpa Pepe stayed with us until Mom was well enough to come home. Her face was a frightening black and blue mess. Neither Mom nor Dad ever told us what had happened. Her face told us all the stories we would ever hear.

I never actually saw Dad beat Mom. There might be a loud fight the night before and scattered bruises on Mom the next day. It was an elephant in the room that none of us kids talked about. Each of us kept our own secrets and nightmares.

WG bought a 1965 two-door olive green Mustang coupe with a black vinyl roof. It was a very cool car, even if it was totally impractical for a family of six. I was on my minibike across the street at Ernie's house. As I headed home, I could see WG coming in my direction also headed home. Suddenly, he pointed the Mustang in my direction and gunned the engine. All I could see was his angry face glaring down at me as the car veered into my lane right at me. In terrified disbelief, I ran my bike into the ditch and WG swerved back into his own lane. I got banged up and was in total shock at what WG had done for no reason.

In terrified confusion I pushed my bike home and made some lame excuse about wrecking the bike. WG glared at me the whole time, but never said a word. I couldn't look him in the eye and escaped to my room as soon as I could. We never talked about that incident but it would haunt me for years. I was so afraid and mad at myself for not being able to stand up to him. Even twenty years later, I could not stand up to him because of my fear.

3

The Hidden Secret

For most of my life, we did not attend church as a family, but for a short period, we attended Our Redeemer Lutheran Church. We attended together. We all got dressed up and Mom even wore a fancy hat. All four of us kids piled in the backseat of the Mustang and off we went to church. I took intense Bible study classes, memorized scriptures, and learned all the books of the Bible in the correct order. There was no profound 'come to Christ' experience, it was just time to get baptized and so I did. I got a Baptismal Certificate and my name was clearly spelled out on it, Rodney Eugene Kendrick.

I even went through the Lutheran Confirmation process. All the facts about Jesus were drilled into my head. I learned the complete church history and doctrine. We studied the different missionary journeys of Paul and the miracles of Jesus. There was never any discussion of a relationship with Jesus. Nobody ever explained what a difference Jesus could make, or if they tried, I never heard it. I learned the catechism that was taught so I could qualify for Confirmation, which I did. After that, we quit going to church just as suddenly as we had started.

That Baptismal Certificate would act as a birth certificate in the years ahead. I was told my original birth certificate had been lost and could not be found. In those days using a baptismal certificate was a common substitute. It was used any time a birth certificate was required. In later years I came to realize that going to church for that short period of time was a way to avoid having to show my real birth certificate, but this was another thing we never talked about, but soon would.

One day while I was kicking around the house, bored and with nothing to do, I started snooping in boxes and drawers in my parents' bedroom. I don't know what I was looking for, I was just curious and looking. Most of the stuff was papers, pictures, and junk. But then I came upon a document that stopped me cold in my tracks. It was a real birth certificate and it was mine, only it couldn't be mine. My name was listed as Rodney Eugene Law and my father was Gene Law.

This could not be right. I had always been Rodney Eugene Kendrick. Mom taught me my name. It was my name the first day of kindergarten, during Little League, and for Boy Scouts. I was stunned as I realized I didn't know who I was. All my life was a lie. WG had always been there, I couldn't remember a time without him. He was there when each of my sisters was born, but what about me? I felt sick to my stomach and dizzy with this new knowledge.

I didn't tell anyone about this. It was my big secret for years. It was a hidden burden and I felt lost. There would come a time when I would be glad that WG was not my father and that I would not have any of his manic-depressive tendencies. But on that day, I was bewildered and lost. I couldn't say I was a victim. I was worse. I was some terrible secret mistake. My father had completely rejected me. Why? What the heck was wrong with me? What did I ever do to him? Inside, I began to harden and outwardly I began to act out. But the hurt, I hid and wouldn't have admitted to anyone.

Years later I would talk with my mother and learn some of her painful truths. This is the story that I would piece together. It isn't complete, but it is as much as I would ever know.

In 1953 my mother was a beautiful teenager, sweet and naive. While still in high school, she entered a swimsuit competition in La Jolla, California, and to her delight and surprise, she won. This brought her sudden popularity with the young men and she was swept off her feet by one of them. She became pregnant and was immediately abandoned by the boy and his family who considered her totally unsuitable for their up-and-coming son.

There was no support for my mother. Nice young girls did not get pregnant. Unmarried girls were forever stigmatized and shamed. There was no DNA testing, no forcing irresponsible men to help financially. At that time boys paid none of the consequences, and girls paid the total price, at least poor girls, from the wrong side of the tracks.

Pregnant girls were forced to leave school as soon as they started to show. If word got out about the pregnancy, they were forced to leave even sooner. Mom transferred to a Catholic school and home for unwed mothers. These girls were separated from family and friends but could finish their education. Most girls gave their babies up for adoption and, if possible, quietly went back to their old lives.

Not my mother. My mother fought to keep me. She loved me. She wanted me and she wasn't about to let me go. It didn't matter that she wasn't married. It only mattered that she kept me. She was determined to do whatever it took to take care of me. I can never understand the shame and humiliation she must have felt. I can only admire her and love her for doing her best. The mother that I remember was tough, determined, and brashly outspoken, except to WG, my father.

Mom married WG while I was still a toddler and they quickly had three more daughters. I grew up calling WG, "Dad." WG worked for Arrowhead Water delivering water to homes and businesses. On the side, he had a tree business and eventually became a certified arborist. He worked on his tree business after hours and on weekends. About the time I hit junior high school, he recruited me to help him with his fledgling tree business. He would cut and trim and I would lug his trimmings to the truck and pile them in. This was hot and dirty work, but it kept me busy and helped my pudgy body go from a young boy to a lean and muscled teenager. This hard work also helped me work off the anger boiling inside of me.

I rode dirt bikes every moment I wasn't working for WG or going to school. I could take out my frustrations by slamming the gears and doing wheelies. We had a pasture for Pinta and that pasture became my running grounds. I'd drive like a wild man through the pasture trying to avoid hitting piles of horse poop. Up one hill and down another, I drove by myself for hours and then dragged myself home exhausted when the sun went down.

I made friends with Jim and John in 7th grade. They were twins and had dirt bikes, too. Between Vista and Oceanside there was an undeveloped area of land that swarmed with dirt bikes. To get to that tract of land I would run my bike on the railroad right of way between trains and the railroad crossings. I would blast across the road laughing at all the cars that were forced to stop and wait for the train. Not me, I was flying with the train and keeping a sharp eye out for the cops. In my mind I was yelling at pursuing cops "Eat my dust." It didn't matter that nobody ever pursued me, it was a favorite game.

I'd meet Jim and John and we would join the wild mob of boys racing through the dusty hills. There was a 200-foot hill to the top of a plateau that was barren and we chased each other and all the other bikers over "Gray Hill". Off to one side was an unfenced avocado orchard and to the west we could see the Pacific Ocean when low smog allowed. I would not appreciate the beauty of that place for years, I only cared how fast my bike would run and who I could beat. I'd go home filthy and pleased with myself every time I went to Gray Hill.

I played Pony League baseball in Junior High School. Mom and WG took me to practice and watched my games. I played left field and catcher when needed. I liked it, it gave me something to do and I was naturally athletic. The girls came because their babysitter was playing baseball (me). I have no idea what the girls did while I played because I was totally into the game, playing as hard as I could. We never played any tournaments and I don't remember ever getting a trophy for playing. There were no participation trophies in those days.

I went to Washington Junior High School and was an A and B student. I did as little as possible to get by in class and still maintain grades that would keep me out of trouble at home. Trouble did find me in 7th grade. That was a tough year.

I was curious and nosey and often tried new things just for the fun of it. My buddies and I rode the school bus and one afternoon on the way home, they dared me to take the handle off of the emergency door at the back. I used a dime as a screwdriver and twist, twist, twist off came the emergency door handle on the back of the school bus. I put the handle back on, but my friends goaded me into taking the handle back off and taking it home. We thought it was hilarious at the time, but I got suspended for three days. They had dared me to do it, but I'm the one who got in trouble. I'm sure I got in trouble at home, but since it was the first time and I can't remember any punishment, it couldn't have been too bad.

The second time I got suspended happened when the biggest bully in school mouthed off at me and gave me a good shove. Fast as lightning I balled up my fist and slammed him as hard as I could in the nose. His nose exploded in a gush of blood. I felt a surge of satisfaction. That was the end of that fight. We both got suspended for three days. That was my second suspension in the first six months of 7th grade and was by far the best suspension experience of junior high school. That bully never mouthed off to me again.

When the class bells rang at the end of the period, there was always a rush for the door and a sea of humanity jammed the halls headed for the next class. The hall monitors were teachers and they could be seen head and shoulders above the rest of the crowd. One day I could see Mr. Reidburger, our principal, down the hall. He was watching all of us and his black-rimmed glasses and coal-black hair were swiveling around looking for trouble in his halls. Stupidly, I screamed out, "Reidburger is a jerk!" He heard me and jerked around, and rapidly plowed through the students looking for the one with the loud mouth. My so-called buddies got as far away from me as they could and ratted me out to "the man." Another three-day suspension went on my record. In fact, I got two three-day suspensions for mouthing off.

Around this time, WG had a belly full of me and my bad behavior and suspensions. One day he and Mom loaded me in the car and off we went for a drive. It was a long boring ride, and we ended up at a military school in Oceanside, California. The school was behind a big gray concrete block wall topped with razor wire. It looked like a prison to me. WG gave me an earful about my unacceptable behavior and threatened that if I got suspended one more time, this is where I would finish school. I couldn't see past the razor wire running around the top of the fence. I decided then and there to keep my nose clean and stay out of trouble. And I did.

Ninth grade started what I would later call my "Glory Years."

I became a Knight at San Marcos High School in San Marcos, California. I participated in football, wrestling, shot put in field and track and ran on a relay team. I played left field on the baseball team. I was a freshman letterman, and I was proud of my performance and skill in athletics.

Our school was so small that we didn't have uniforms for all of the baseball players. We had to run sprints and the fastest runners got to wear the uniforms and play. It didn't matter how well we played baseball in practice, winners were the ones who played. Usually, I outsprinted everyone and got to play, but I wanted to get a uniform because I played ball good enough to earn the spot, not because I could outsprint everyone.

I was not in the elite in-crowd in high school and did not attract those cool, hot chicks from that crowd. I had lots of dates, but no sweethearts. There was one memorable date in ninth grade, my very first date ever. Mom and Dad drove us in the Mustang because I was too young to drive. I took Marilyn to see Iron Butterfly in San Diego. Every big band came to Southern California, but Iron Butterfly was at the top of my list and had just released their giant smash hit In-A-Gadda-Da-Vida. That hit song blared all 17 minutes with its long drum solo and I felt on top of the world. When we took Marilyn home, I walked her to the front door and planned to give her a kiss, but Mom and Dad were in the car and I was too embarrassed. It was still a great first date.

Tenth grade opened a new world for me. I was 17 and could legally drive in California. WG bought a car that became my car for school and so I could participate in athletics and all of the required athletic practices. Instead of paying me to work for him, he paid for the car, insurance and gasoline.

The car was a 1957 silver and black Chevy Bel Air. The car had been totally restored, mag wheels and Goodyear polyglass tires with raised white letters. The interior was black tuck and roll vinyl which looked new. It had a Borg-Warner T-10 four-speed transmission, a Corvette 327 engine and 30-30 cam which made the engine thump (sound like a Harley). It was love at first sight, except that there was a huge burned and rusted circle in the center of the hood. There had been a fire in the engine and all that damage needed to be fixed. I took on the job, did the repairs and when finished WG had the hood repainted. I was proud of that car and would never have to let Mom and Dad drive me on a date again.

Between my car and sports, I had a happy sophomore year. My grades came up and I stayed out of trouble. I was looking forward to the next two years of high school. WG was his usual self, but there was the car that he provided, the gas and insurance and spending money. I didn't want to rock that boat.

And then my world fell out beneath me. I was informed we were moving to Jackson, Mississippi, a world away from beautiful Southern California, gorgeous beaches, and all my hopes for the future. There was no family discussion about why we were moving. We were told we were moving close to WG's mother and that was that. As usual his orders were given and obeyed by us without question.

I was furious. I did not want to leave Southern California to go to Mississippi. It sounded like the end of the world to me and not the least bit cool. Everything that was important was happening in Southern California in the 1970s. I hoped to be a star athlete in high school. I couldn't see that anything good was going to happen for me in Mississippi. No friends, no athletics, no girlfriends, nothing. I was blue and in shock. I could think of a thousand reasons not to go to Mississippi. It was sweltering hot and humid. The beaches were 90 miles to the south of Jackson. I knew not a single person except for Grandmother Mae T, and she was different from anyone I had ever known. She was Southern Baptist and prayed out loud over every meal, something we never, ever did. She prayed that we would all get saved, and that Jesus would bless her son's tree business.

In reality, we had no choice about our move. Jesus had not blessed WG's business in California. He had a major contract with a golf course that owed him a lot of money for services rendered. When they refused to pay, WG lost just about everything he had. He thought he would have a better chance if he took his business to Mississippi. For him it was a move back home. For me it was like falling off a cliff and waking up in The Twilight Zone.

Moving was an ugly and embarrassing transition. Mom and WG loaded up his 2-½ ton white Chevy work truck, the last piece of equipment he was able to hang on to. Everything we owned was piled in the back of that truck and covered with a blue tarp. The family El Camino was towed behind the truck and the back of it was as full as the Chevy. If there had been a rocking chair tied on top of the blue tarp, it would have looked just like the Beverly Hillbillies making their move. I was embarrassed beyond words, but at least I was driving behind them. The girls were all loaded on a plane and flown to Mississippi where Grandma Mae T picked them up and took care of them until we got there.

I followed behind in my very cool 1957 silver and black Chevy Bel Air and pretended we were not traveling together. My Bel Air was a hot rod in every sense of the word. As we left California and entered hilly country, the Hillbilly truck ahead would stagger up the inclines. Eventually, it was going so slow I could have outwalked it. I would slow down and let them get way ahead of me. Then I would hit the gas and run through the gears to catch up with them. My game of "slow down and speed up" entertained me until we hit the desert.

The desert was hot, flat and dry. Driving my unairconditioned car became a test of endurance, and it was a test for my parents ahead. Their truck wasn't air-conditioned either. For a short time, the cacti and the roadrunners were interesting, but soon the heat of the day drained all joy out of the drive and it became a miserable hot, dusty drive without end. Soon into this cross-country trek WG mercifully decided we would drive at night and sleep in the heat of the day. The air-conditioned motel rooms were a blessing from the desert heat, and those few that did have pools, I enjoyed.

The days ran together across the states of SE California, Arizona, New Mexico, and the western arm of Texas.

Somewhere around Odessa, we drove through the weirdest storm I have ever experienced. Lightning was thick in the sky and ran horizontal to the earth. There was so much lightning that the hair on my whole body stood on end and tingled. There was no rain, but even the air smelled of lightning. I have never forgotten this storm and the only people I have ever met who knew what I was talking about were other Texans who called it a "lightning storm." Eventually, we drove out of it somewhere in the Dallas area.

East of Dallas we returned to the land of green and increasing humidity. The rest of the drive was without incident and we finally drove into Jackson, Mississippi.

4

CULTURE SHOCK, POT, AND JESUS

Mississippi was shocking to me. The weather with its horrible high humidity kept me in a dripping sweat all day long and most of every night. The never-ending noise of the cicadas and the buzz of biting mosquitoes was miserable. It was August and the heat and the bugs were at their very worst. The lightning bugs were fun, but that novelty instantly vanished with the first mosquito bite of the night. Thank goodness school was starting soon.

Starting a new school is always intimidating, but I was the blue-eyed, long-haired California transfer. My silver and black '57 Chevy and my cool attitude would make me a welcome addition to the class of 1972. Or so I thought.

I strutted into Forest Hill High School thinking I would show all the hicks and chicks what cool was all about. As I was sitting in the homeroom that first morning, the vice-principal, Mrs. Ferguson, paged me over the intercom inviting me to come immediately to her office. What was this all about? I strutted down the hallway thinking I was about to get a warm, personal welcome from the vice-principal herself.

The first thing she said to me was, "What do you mean coming to school looking like that?" She stood glaring at me. I didn't know what she was talking about. I had on my coolest California duds and my long hair was neat and tidy. I was dumbfounded and stood there like a moron. Finally, I shrugged, I didn't know what to say, but she sure did.

"The dress code at Forest Hill High School requires that boys have their hair off their collars and off their ears. Cut short, young man. Do you understand? Go home and don't come back until your hair meets the dress code." she dismissed me with a wave of her hand.

I walked out of the school that morning in disbelief. There were no long-hair bans in California. Surely, this was some mistake, some idiotic ruling that would not apply to me. I loved my long sun-bleached hair and was not going to cut it off because of some stupid school rule.

When I got home Mom and I had a good laugh about it. She couldn't believe the school would have such a stupid rule, either. But, after a long discussion and lots of complaining on my part, she sided with the school. I thought to myself, welcome to Mississippi. I left to get my haircut and started a list of complaints in my head about the injustice of this forced move to such a backward hick state.

It never occurred to me that being publicly humiliated by the school administration would make me popular at school. My hair may have been properly short, but I was still the golden transfer from California and my classmates accepted me as part cool and part renegade bad boy. Back home I had been considered a jock. I had played football, baseball, wrestled and been part of the track team. I had lettered, but even so, playing sports had a lot more to do with having fun with my buddies than it did about any great talent on my part. Here things were different, I didn't have any buddies and I didn't care. Football lost all its appeal because of the staggering heat and humidity. No way did I want to participate in that. In fact, looking back I am surprised that Mom and WG didn't give me a hard time about dropping sports, but they didn't.

Without sports I did not fit into the in-crowd. The prettiest girls belonged there, and I wasn't interested in anything but the very prettiest girls. There were other things I wanted more than a pretty date. There were rebels that I had left behind in California. They were the ones who pursued sex, drugs and rock and roll. Those things had a lot more appeal to me at the time.

Back in the early seventies, marijuana grew wild and was dirt cheap. I never paid for it. It was available in abundance and everyone shared their stash with me. It took the edge off my anger issues and covered up a lot of deeply held hurts that I carefully nursed. This was another thing my folks never confronted me about. I'm not sure they ever knew I was smoking marijuana, but smoke I did.

The Bible Belt was alive and thriving in Mississippi. Our Principal, Mr. Walker, would broadcast a devotion over the intercom every morning at 8 AM. He read from the Bible and prayed for every student in school that day. At first I was shocked. California never had devotions, there was never any mention of God over the intercom and certainly no prayers.

Mr. Walker's devotions were my first introduction to a personal God and daily prayer. He encouraged us to invite God into the school, into our hearts and into our lives. Later, I would see these morning devotions as the beginning of a genuine relationship with God. For the time being, I was chasing sex, drugs and rock and roll. Mr. Walker's devotions were far, far away from my heart and my good times. They were just another part of the weirdness of Mississippi.

Every Friday and Saturday night my buddies and I would join in illegal street drag racing. We would go out by the airport to a remote stretch of blacktop and race. My Chevy held its own with that crowd. Sometimes I lost, sometimes I won. The rich kids raced for money; I only raced for bragging rights and as a reason to attract chicks.

It seems like all teens have a driving ritual that involves cruising from one end of town to another on Friday and Saturday nights. The Rebels of Forest Hill cruised through the parking lot of Shoney's. We would drive aimlessly looking for pretty girls to talk to and impress. Me, I was on the lookout for Chicks. Chicks are what we call pretty girls back home on the West Coast. My Jackson friends thought this was priceless and nicknamed me "Chick." I became known as "Chick that goes to Forest Hill." I thought at first, they were making fun of me, like I was a cross-dresser or something. In reality, they thought I was cooler than they were and it was their way of paying homage. If I had known that I would have been flattered.

My day-to-day memories of high school are a little hazy, partly from smoking pot, and partly because I just wanted to get through it. I took all the usual classes required for a student to get into college. I made decent grades, but nothing spectacular. I did not apply myself in school because it was boring. I dated, but there was no special girlfriend for me. I worked for WG consistently and stayed fit and trim, full of complaints about how hot and dirty the work was. WG turned a deaf ear to my griping, but I always had money for gas and the occasional date.

I did want to go to both my junior and senior proms. I met a girl named Debbie in one of my classes. She was a cute girl with long brown hair and big brown eyes that she could twitch back and forth in unison. This silly trait and her easy smile were attractive and I decided she was the one to take to the junior prom. I made plans to get to know her better.

I spent a lot of time with Alex who lived around the corner from Debbie. Alex was a friend I often smoked pot with and who the police knew by name. He had been picked up a time or two, nothing serious, but he had a reputation. I never considered that his reputation might have been pretty bad in his own neighborhood.

One afternoon I ambled over to chat with Debbie and she was her usual warm, sweet self. We talked and laughed about nothing for the next couple of hours. Eventually, when I felt brave enough, I casually invited her to the prom. My mouth dried up while I waited for her to say yes, but she didn't. She sat quietly looking down at the flower bed.

She hesitated and then sadly said, "My father will never let me go out with you. Never. Never under any circumstances will he let me date you. You hang around with Alex, and I'm not allowed to even talk to him."

I could not believe my ears. I was crushed and furious at the same time. I could not think of a response. So, I got up and kept my mouth shut. I never asked her why her dad would feel that way. I never thought to go talk directly to Debbie's dad, man to man. Facing him was scarier than facing WG. It just wasn't in me. So, I looked at pretty Debbie's sad face, shoved my hands in my pockets and walked away. I never looked back, never spoke to her again.

Now, years later, I understand how her dad felt. I was friends with a known pothead, so I must be a pothead. Of course, I was but I thought my secret was safe. That birds of a feather flocking together business didn't mean a thing to me. I had never been in trouble, in or out of school (at least not in Mississippi), my grades were decent and I only had one speeding ticket (even though I deserved a lot of speeding and racing tickets, I had managed to avoid the law). In my mind I was the ideal guy to date his daughter. Heck, I was the ideal guy to date anybody's daughter, even my mom would agree with that.

It also never occurred to me that my not knowing Jesus could be a reason for rejection. At the time it was just another painful rejection and the reason didn't matter at all. I did not go to either the Junior or the Senior Prom. For the rest of high school, all of my dates were casual, and I never let another girl get close. I built layer upon layer of wall around my heart for protection.

I had lots of walls by this time. But, I was also a Junior in high school and subject to teenage hormones. I had sworn off girls, but by the next week I found myself attracted to a blue-eyed blond, named Linda who was from a rival school. I had no intention of getting close to her, but she was attractive and flirty. She invited me to a Campus Life meeting. I had no idea what that was so said "yes" to her for the fun of it. Little did I know that one big wall would come down that night and it would have nothing to do with a pretty girl.

It was the Monday night before Easter and Linda and I went to her friend's home. The meeting started with snacks and fellowship and me flirting with the cute girl who had invited me. A guy named Eddie introduced himself as the leader of Campus Life and explained that he was a college student at Mississippi College. He explained that Campus Life was a branch of Youth for Christ that evangelized at the high school level.

We got comfortable and sat in a large circle. The meeting was opened with prayer. Then each person shared how Jesus had interacted with them in their lives during the past week. They all seemed to have some point where Jesus had kept them out of trouble or helped them make good decisions. They talked as though Jesus was their best friend and that he had given them personal advice to get through the week. When it was my turn, I passed. I didn't have a thing to say. I had been baptized and confirmed, but Jesus wasn't my friend. I didn't know him at all, at least not like everyone in this circle seemed to know him. I felt like a freak in a circus sideshow.

When the meeting mercifully ended, Eddie looked me in the eyes and said, "God loves you and He has a plan for your life." He said it with such conviction that I was immediately drawn in. I didn't have a plan for my life. I didn't have a clue what I was going to do tomorrow, how could God? Just the idea that God could have a plan for my life got my interest. I found myself suddenly eager to hear more.

As I leaned in to listen to Eddie, he opened his Bible and turned to the book of Romans. He had me read Romans 3:23 aloud, which said,

"For all have sinned and fall short of the glory of God." (NKJV)

I thought, that's for sure! Especially me! I had known this truth every day of my life.

Then Eddie explained that we have all missed the mark in God's eyes. All of us have sinned. Every. Single. One. I for sure knew that I sinned. I knew that WG was another big hateful sinner. There were lots of sinners, but I thought there were some people a lot holier than me who didn't sin. Eddie explained that Jesus Christ was the only one who ever walked on this earth who didn't sin. That statement I could believe.

Eddie continued finding scriptures but handed me the Bible to read for myself. I didn't know it at the time, but he was walking me down the pure and beautiful "Roman Road."

> "For the wages of sin is death, but the gift of God is eternal life in Christ Jesus our Lord." Romans 6:23. (NKJV)

Eddie went on to say that our sin separates us from God. We cannot do anything to bring fellowship with God without accepting that God sent Jesus to die for each one of us.

Next was Romans 5:8

> "But God demonstrates His own love toward us, in that while we were still sinners, Christ died for us." (NKJV)

Eddie explained that eternal life came to man because Jesus Christ died on the cross of each of us. I may not have fully understood what his sacrifice meant, but I could understand that Jesus had made one big sacrifice to save me. I didn't know him, but he must have known me.

The only father I had ever known was WG and if he ever really loved me, I didn't know it. I thought about the man who had run my bike off of the road and laughed about it. The man who poured water and crawdads on my little face. Now, I was hearing about someone I didn't know who had died on a cross for me out of love. I felt my heart soften at this thought.

Eddie continued to Romans 10:9 and again handed the Bible to me to read,

> "That if you confess with your mouth the Lord Jesus and believe in your heart that God has raised Him from

the dead, you will be saved." (NKJV)

Eddie simply asked me, "Do you want to ask Jesus to be Lord and Savior of your life?" My mind raced through the mess of my life, the many times I felt unloved and abandoned. I thought of all the hurts deep inside and the rage that was never far below the surface of my skin.

We weren't in a church. We were surrounded by people, but I saw none of them. I forgot that I came because of a girl I hardly knew. I simply felt the presence of God and everything else around me melted into a blur. Most of all, I felt peace and a sense of hope that I had never experienced before. I answered Eddie with a quiet "yes" and he led me through what I now know as the Sinner's Prayer of Repentance.

My salvation experience did not involve any bright lights or visions. There were no thunderclaps of emotion. Earlier in the night, our group had sung "It is Well with my Soul," and the words of that song floated through my mind and I found myself feeling that peace and the sweet presence of God.

There were wonderful, comforting words to be found in the Bible, and I wanted to know what they were. I had a thirst to know Jesus, the Holy Spirit, and all of the other secrets hidden in the Word of God. I read my Bible every night and developed a tender fellowship that I shared with no one.

I was quietly baptized at the Daniel Memorial Baptist Church. I can't even remember if my mother and WG came. My life moved two steps forward and one step back for me throughout the rest of high school.

I had a close friend named Jay. One day Jay was at my house and found a picture of me when I was about nine. I had a flat top, buzzed to the skin on the sides and one inch on top, flat as a landing field. He thought this would be a great look for graduation. I didn't want to do that, but he coaxed me into it as a protest the stupid and outdated dress code. By the end of the night, we had shaved each other's heads and were bald as billiard balls.

The next day at school, we fully expected to be called into the office. Our friends thought it was a riot to poke the nose of the establishment, but apparently the establishment thought we looked great. Not a word was ever said to either of us by anyone in the administration, and thankfully, our hair grew out enough by graduation that we weren't embarrassed.

5

THE RUNNING YEARS

After graduation from high school, I took a trip back to California to visit with the Thompson twins. I sold my Chevy after graduation and bought a Volkswagen Beetle. The VW wasn't air conditioned, either, but it was easier on gasoline. It was a long, hot drive to California, but I did it in two days and slept in the car one night.

The twins, Jim and John, were dirt biker buddies from junior high school. Visiting the Thompson family was like going to the circus. There were six boys in the family and there was always something going on in every corner of the house. For all the chaos, it was still organized. Each kid was expected to contribute to the family in a tangible way, either by doing chores or getting a job and contributing money. That included me.

I got a job with the Vista Unified School District in the maintenance department. I helped clean and service the boilers in the furnaces for the heating system. It was interesting work that was extremely dirty. I would go home (back to the Thompson's) covered in black soot from head to toe every day. We were not required to wear any safety gear and I blew black snot the entire summer. Every day I would hop in the shower and scrub from head to toe while the water ran off my body like ink down the drain. This helped me contribute a little money each month and pay my way.

Then, Jim, John and I would hang out. We would talk and go cruising. We made many runs to the A&W. Then, almost every weekend, I would hit the beach.

The twins were not into surfing, but that didn't keep me from buying a surfboard and going without them. I would hit the cold Pacific water and I learned to surf like the beginner I was. I watched other surfers and did my best to do what they did. I made progress, but I would always be a beginner.

In this casual way, the summer passed quickly. When it was time to leave, I left my surfboard at a shop that eventually sold it on consignment. I thanked the twins for a great summer and headed East through the desert toward Mississippi. Along the way, I contemplated my future.

College seemed like the logical choice. I did not want to keep working for my stepdad. That work was hot, sweaty manual labor. His constant nit-picking was discouraging and there were days when I downright hated the work and hated him, too, for that matter.

As it turned out, WG was all for me going to college and was willing to finance my education. I enrolled at Hinds Junior College in Raymond, Mississippi. The college was about twenty miles SW of Jackson on highway 18. I commuted that first year. My freshman year seemed like Grade 13, and not like college at all. Classes were doable, and I made A's and B's. I kept working part time for WG.

My sophomore year was a refreshing change for me as I moved to Raymond and lived in the dorm away from the thumb of my micromanaging stepdad. I was assigned a roommate and I was concerned that I would end up living with a slob who would irritate me every minute. That didn't happen. My roommate was just like me in a lot of ways. He was a young kid away from home for the first time and looking for a place to fit in until he could figure out what he wanted to do for the rest of his life.

I was very fortunate in that WG paid for all my tuition, books and room and board. I ate in the cafeteria, I did not have to work to get through college. I did have to maintain decent grades. Looking back years later, I can see that he tried his best to do right by me. He gave me a chance to be something besides his free labor. I was never really his free labor. I always had a few bucks in my pocket. He bought cars for me and paid the insurance. I always had gas money. He never gave me an actual paycheck, so I never knew what I had earned with my hard work. He paid me when and however much he wanted, so I felt he never treated me right. I had so many resentments toward him that I could not see any good, only the bad.

I enjoyed the freedom of living on my own, but I had a hard time finding a place to fit in. There was a Baptist Student Union on campus, but it was very cliquish. I visited several times, but

I never made a connection. This was a new unpleasant experience for me. Before, I had been generally liked and welcomed wherever I went. I don't know if all the connections were made as Freshmen, and newcomers were too much work to bother with. Whatever the reason, after a few tries to make friends, I quit going.

I went home on weekends. Just like every other student on the planet, I dragged all my dirty clothes home. Mom insisted that she do my laundry, so I happily left it with her. She fed me while I was at home and I relished her meals. Sometimes, I worked for WG, but not every weekend. He didn't seem to expect it and I was glad to be out from under.

I went to church at home in Jackson. This allowed me to keep some connection with Jesus, but I was drifting away without realizing it. I wasn't reading my Bible as much. The lure of the world was enticing, and like a great many college students, there were more interesting things going on than God.

I got my Associates Degree, but still couldn't decide on a major. Until I decided, there was no point in going to a four-year school. I moved back home. I started my own business.

The City of Crystal Springs, MS was expanding their tax base and running new water lines outside of their city limits. They would run the line and put a meter in front of every house. I followed behind them and offered to dig a trench and lay the line to connect each house to city water. I saw this as my "gold mine" opportunity.

I rented an old, white Ford 150 pickup that came with a trailer and a Ditch Witch to do the trenching. I got this equipment from a friend of WG, which should have been my first red flag. I loaded up with PVC pipe and fittings to make the water connections.

Making sales was surprisingly easy. I followed behind the trucks laying the main lines and knocked on every door those lines passed. Everyone wanted to be hooked up to a clean water supply. They might water the grass with rust-tinged well water, but fresh city water was enormously appealing. I would knock on a door and often face a middle-aged person, who wanted the water but didn't want to lay the line themselves. We'd chat about where to put the line and I'd give them a by-the-foot price. We'd shake on it and on to the next door I would go.

What I didn't know was that my most important piece of equipment, the old Ditch Witch, was completely worn out. It spent more time in the shop than it did working for me. The owner paid for all the repairs as I was paying him rent for a working machine. I couldn't afford to buy my own new Ditch Witch, which is a good thing, or I might never have gone back to school.

I soon realized that I would never make good money because I couldn't work half the time. In fact, I was going down the drain financially faster than I thought possible. After three frustrating months, I closed the business before I got so far down the hole I could never get out.

For the rest of that year, I worked the tree business for WG and thought about a real career. My dream job was to be a park ranger at a National Park. After doing a lot of research, I discovered that the prerequisites were long and political. It would require years of prior work experience and a recommendation from a US Representative. This became a pie in the sky dream for me, but that still left State Parks as an option.

The University of Southern Mississippi at Hattiesburg offered a degree in Outdoor Recreation and Resource Management. I wanted to work in a park, any park. That was the dream. I wanted to be outside and have no confines. I moved to Hattiesburg, enrolled at USM and finally, declared a major.

Junior college helped me get all the boring required classes under my belt. Getting that work done had been a grind and a matter of just "get 'er done." Until now, my grades had been acceptable. In elementary school I got lots of comments, like "doesn't apply himself". School was boring to me. I was often the clown of the class when I was young. I could not sit still. Recess was the only fun class I ever took. High school wasn't much different. My grades were good enough to keep me out of trouble, but I was never engaged in learning anything. USM offered something I was not expecting. Classes were challenging and interesting. Somewhere in my head, a lightbulb clicked on.

For the first time in my life, I excelled. I maintained a 4.0 grade average in my declared field of study. I was forced to think. I learned how to take great notes and apply myself. I learned how to regurgitate required answers. Nobody tells you that, but it is a fact of life. Getting good grades in school means learning to pick out the important information from the side notes and stories that college professors often spew out. It is also a fact that you must roll out of bed, suit up and show up every day for every class. I did everything required and did it because I was finally engaged in learning. I would graduate magna cum laude and be hailed as a scholar at my first park job (which absolutely delighted both of my parents and me).

This is not to say that I wasn't involved in anything else during those college years. I had a girlfriend named Melanie. We dated for the last two years of college. She finally dumped me when I wouldn't quit nagging her about smoking. My parents both smoked and stunk to high heaven when I was a kid. I smelled like a smoker myself. It's a wonder I didn't develop lung cancer from all the secondhand smoke. I hated that habit in Melanie and kissing her was like licking a dirty ashtray. It's really no wonder that she dumped me. I can nag with the best of them when something bugs me.

I kicked around with guys who liked to canoe on the Okatoma Creek. The water was clear and beautiful, perfect for lazy paddling and drinking beer. The scenery was green and lush. When the heat and humidity got to us, we'd stop and swim.

My senior year of college, I moved out of the dorm into a house, which became party central. My roommate had a reel-to-reel recorder and the Almond Brothers played 24 hours a day. The TV was on all the time, too, but with no sound. It seemed normal to watch the picture and listen to the music, everybody was doing that. The refrigerator was always stocked with beer, but almost no food. Friends were welcome to come and go as they pleased. There was a party literally every night of the week.

God was far away in Hattiesburg. I did not go to church. I wasn't reading my Bible. I wasn't living any kind of Godly life. My time was full of fun and God was not important. I might have an occasional stab of guilt, but mostly, God left me alone to do my own thing. That suited me fine. Without WG and God to force me into submission, I was totally free to run any direction I wanted to go. Run, I did, both figuratively and literally.

During my senior year at USM I took a stress test. The results were not what I expected. After working all those years hauling brush and laboring beside WG, I expected that I would be in excellent shape. Not so. My report came back saying that I was only in "fair" condition. The beer and the partying had taken a toll on my body. This was totally unacceptable to me and I did everything I could to change that. I started jogging and did it every day, slowly increasing distance. Over time, I progressed to three miles a day then five miles a day. Eventually I would run five miles in thirty minutes or so and I did that faithfully from then on. I loved feeling like a healthy animal and the runner's high was as good as any drug I had ever used with no side effects or hangovers.

During a winter school break, I took a diving trip to Belize. The trip was sponsored by USM and organized by Dr. Burchell, who was a professor in the Recreation and Resource Management Department. We went as a sponsored group and all costs (except booze) were included, even a side trip to the Mayan Ruins.

We flew into Guatemala City on TACA Airlines and landed at the airport. We were met and surrounded by soldiers in green camouflage carrying AK-47s. None of us were prepared for this and immediately felt apprehensive and nervous. These men patrolled the entire airport area, checked our passports and luggage, and stamped our Visas. Then, without incident, we boarded a prop plane headed for San Pedro Island in Belize.

There were no paved roads on San Pedro Island when we were there. When I looked out the window and saw a sand runway, I panicked. I was afraid we would all get killed on landing, but we didn't. We landed on that sand runway which was as scary as the armed guards we had left behind. I was sure the plane would sink in the sand, but it didn't and we landed safely.

We got off the plane and checked into our accommodations. The rooms weren't air-conditioned but had fans that were cool enough to get by. The food was delicious and I had lobster every single night. It was a romantic environment with music, dancing and walks along the moonlit beach.

Melanie and I were still together at this time and one night she and I strolled out to the end of a pier. It led out into the water about fifty feet from shore. We sat down at the end of the pier and eventually we laid down and looked up. As we gazed up we saw millions of stars. There were no bright city lights, no nearby neon lights to compete with the sky, only the stars themselves filled the sky from horizon to horizon. There were so many stars that at first. I couldn't find the Big Dipper. It was another one of many magical moments that were to be found at that time and in that place. I was struck with the wonder of it, without giving God any of the glory for creating it.

    One of the days we were on San Pedro Island, we took a day to tour the Mayan ruins of Belize. The ruins were dotted throughout Belize and at times the city and the ruins commingled. We were astounded to see open sewers, meat markets and street vendors in such close proximity. The overwhelming stench of the sewers combined with the mouthwatering smells of the street food and the sight of raw meat hanging over the sewers ruined any chance of eating a bite on this side trip. My day was spent fighting my gag reflex for control.

In spite of that, we explored the ruins, climbing where allowed, and hiking throughout the area. I did experience awe at the Mayan people who were able to move and place such huge granite blocks without the benefit of modern machinery. Each block was carefully placed without mortar or cement to hold them, and now, hundreds of years later, they are still in place. Just like the Egyptian pyramids, the Mayan ruins astound modern man. While the colors and the sites were glorious, my most vivid recollections of that trip with open sewers in the streets.

Back in San Pedro, I looked forward to the SCUBA classes I had signed up for. The lessons were more of a "how not to kill yourself" session than actual lessons. We learned the bare basics, but the entire lesson was less than half an hour. We did have excellent guides who knew the waters and none of us dove alone, so I felt safer.

I was not prepared for the breath-taking beauty found underwater. The colorful pictures shown in National Geographic paled in comparison to the reality of the reef before me. All the different shades of red, pink, orange and green of the corals were a surprise. The exotic beauty of the marine life left me with sensory overload. Swimming and exploring swept away the time.

I saw a nurse shark that was as big as Jaws, at least in my own mind. It swam around for a while scaring me, but never got too close. Eventually, it swam off, but I stayed alert for its return the rest of the dive. On the boat I regaled the other divers with the story of this huge shark. The guides roared with laughter, because the shark was actually much smaller than I described. They had seen it, and said it might have been 12' long, but not an inch more than that. Then, they teased me about Jaws coming to get me for the rest of that dive.

Another time we dove to the edge of the continental shelf. The sandy bottom of the beach sloped gently down and we explored the wildlife and corals as we went. It was a leisurely descent and none of us were in a hurry. I cut my knee on a coral and it began to bleed. It stung from the salt water, but not enough to quit the dive. As we descended the color of my blood began to change until close to the continental shelf, it turned black. It was creepy, but I found out later that it was normal. Colors do change the deeper you dive. Looking out over the edge of the shelf, everything was black and forbidding. Nothing like the beauty of shallower depths was evident. I couldn't see my hand in front of my face, and thankfully, we did not tarry at the edge for long. Coming up we stopped twice to decompress, but the stops were short and none of us had any decompression problems.

My time in Belize could have been spent getting closer to God. I was surrounded by His beauty and glory everywhere I looked, from the lazy blue sky to the azure waters teeming with his colorful creatures, and the lush green beauty of the island itself. I was sidetracked by Melanie, by my friends, by my own lack of interest in anything beyond my own senses. I was surrounded by God's grandeur and oblivious to his perfection.

6

Working

A few days after getting home, I doubled over with intense abdominal pain. Mom and WG drove me to St. Dominic Hospital in Jackson, MS. The hospital determined that I was severely dehydrated and my body had developed at least one kidney stone because of it. Leritine was administered to control my excruciating pain and as I drifted off to sleep, my body reacted to the Leritine. When my face turned blue, my stepdad alerted the nurse. I had coded.

I was in complete peace and floated on my back in a dark tunnel. I had no discomfort, no pain. When I looked at my feet, I could see a brilliant light at the end of the tunnel. I felt soothed and relaxed.

I was startled awake to the concerned faces of hospital staff hovering around me. One person had electro-shock paddles in his hand. I realized my heart had stopped and panic immediately grabbed me. I remember crying over and over, "I don't want to die. I don't want to die." I was a wild mix of emotions.

I had felt perfectly safe and at peace, but the instant I woke up, I was terrified.

The hospital pumped me full of electrolytes and water. I did pass a kidney stone while there, and that eased the pain considerably. Eventually I went home feeling much better, with a stern warning to hydrate better and to stay away from Leritine. I was reminded to be thankful that I didn't pass a kidney stone while on my bike miles from any hospital.

When I got home, I began looking for a job in earnest. I could always go back to dragging brush for WG, but that was the last thing I wanted to do. I had a college degree and had, in fact, graduated cum laude, much to my delight. I did not, not, not want to go back to manual labor. I scoured the papers for ads looking for work in any state park, but there were none. I was discouraged by the ads that were posted, and dragging brush began to look like my default option.

When I was about to give up the job search and settle for brush hauling, I found an ad looking for a salesperson/manager at a backpacking and camping supply store in Jackson. It would be an inside job with A/C in the summer and heat in the winter. I was certainly qualified. While I was ecstatic that I wouldn't have to work for WG, I was also honest with the supply store. I wanted to work in the park system and they were willing to hire me until that time came several months later.

I kept searching for ads in the State Park System and eventually I found an opening at Tombigbee State Park. The position was for an Assistant Park Manager. I called and got an interview. In late summer of 1978, I made the trip once again up the Natchez Trace to Tombigbee Park. I drove my 1968 cabover van and it was a nostalgic drive in comparison to the year before when I had pedaled my way. The Park was constructed in the thirties by the Civilian Conservation Corps, which was part of the "New Deal" program used to stimulate the economy after the stock market crash of 1929. I pulled into the park full of the hope that this job offered.

Long story short, they hired me as an Assistant Manager. My salary included a log cabin in the park with all utilities paid. I was hired as a 24/7 park employee with every other weekend off. I was given a park vehicle for use while working.

The park also sent a story to the area newspaper saying that they were delighted to announce that they had been able to hire an honor graduate (scholar was the word used) to work in the park. I thought that was nice of them, and my mother was ecstatic over the article. Years later after she died, I would find that article carefully tucked away with her mementoes. I was more touched at finding the article with her things than the original printing.

Tombigbee is a large park with access to the lake and boat docks, individual camping sites, a large group camp that had a cook staff and a wait staff for summer camps and a park concession stand. There was a full staff of day and night park rangers that collected fees and enforced the park rules. Only the Manager and I lived on site. I thought I had found my dream job and eagerly moved into my cabin.

My job duties were varied and included collecting fees, making deposits and helping people find where they wanted to go. All of these duties were carefully explained during the interview and I looked forward to this new adventure. I hoped it would become a stepping stone to working in a big national park.

What wasn't explained during the interview process turned my dream job into a living nightmare. My parked vehicle in front of my cabin was like a neon sign to my front door. Even in the middle of the night with all lights out, campers would bang on my door for their "urgent" business.

"The coke machine ate my quarter."

"My car won't start."

"When does the office open?"

"Can you give me change for the vending machine?"

"Where is the closest restaurant?"

"When can I rent a canoe?"

"Can I rent a paddleboat here?"

And my very favorite question of all time, "The toilets are clogged up, will you come and fix them?"

All this nonsense would have been laughable if I'd been able to sleep any night all the way through. Each day was busy with park duties and every night was filled with banging on the door.

Finally, the summer ended and the chaos came to a screeching halt. In its place came abject winter boredom. There were very few campers in the park during the winter and even fewer visitors. All the part-time summer help was laid off. I piddled around during the day and often visited the maintenance shop where all park vehicles were maintained. I would chat and visit and occasionally turn a wrench to help.

After the craziness of the summer, I thought I would be happy with the peace and quiet of winter. Instead, I found myself restless and disappointed that what I worked so hard to achieve was not what I wanted to do at all. As Spring approached, I knew I did not want another summer like the last one. I gave proper notice and left. I still wanted to work outside in the open, but I no longer wanted to be a park ranger.

A transmission powerline construction company hired me and a new chapter opened. I was based out of Mississippi but was sent to construction sites in other states. I was hired as an Assistant to the Superintendent and wherever he was assigned, I moved with him. I answered to the Superintendent but worked with all the different specialized crews. My job was to document the progress of each day's work on the power lines being installed. I was responsible for creating and maintaining a wall chart that tracked the progress of completion of each job. This was a challenging job and I found myself well-suited to it. I liked the work. I liked the different crew members. I was content.

I was soon promoted to Materials Specialist. I documented and inventoried all materials needed for each project. Each job site was unique and there were hundreds of parts and materials to track.

There were multiple job crews for each site, each with their own specialized area. There was a foundation crew, an assembly crew, an erection crew and the wire pulling crew. Each crew came and left according to their assignment on the job. We became a working family. We worked hard during the day and even harder at night partying to the max, and drinking. I was transferred multiple times, and it was the same with every crew I worked with.

I worked in Belle Glade, Florida, and before that project was complete, I was transferred to Waverly, Ohio. My superintendent completed the job that we were on and I was transferred to Pine Bluff, Arkansas. Six months later, I was transferred to New Hebron, MS.

On a September evening, I hopped into my Camaro with plans to run to Purvis and eat supper with a local girlfriend and her parents. I only made it half-way there before I fell asleep at the wheel and crashed.

7

Hurt, Doubt and Confusion

I woke up with my feet and legs in agony. I was disoriented. I looked around and could see that I was in a hospital. I didn't know where. All I could feel was my pain and I cried out. A male nurse came to me.

"Mr. Kendrick, are you finally awake? How are you feeling? What can I help you with?" he asked.

"My legs and my feet are killing me." I cried.

Very matter of factly and with no compassion, he replied, "Your feet and legs are gone. Look for yourself. I'll get you something for pain" and he flipped the sheets back as he casually walked out of the room.

I looked in stunned disbelief at where my feet and legs should have been, and there was nothing except white bandaging. I felt nauseated and sick inside as the truth of what he said washed over me. Despair overwhelmed me. I was totally lost. Disconnected. Shocked. I couldn't think. I couldn't comprehend anything at the time except there was nothing where my legs and feet should have been. My life was over. Then I slept.

When I woke up there was a relentless heavy chaos in my mind. My legs were gone and my whole life was lost. My mind finally registered that I would never run. I would never again ride a bicycle. I would never hike from one tower line to the next at work. I would never swing a pretty girl around the dance floor. The only thing I could think of was everything I could never do again. I disconnected and could not communicate with family or the hospital staff for a time. I denied. I screamed at God for doing this to me. And, finally, I slept again.

My life was meaningless without the ability to walk and run. I would rather be dead than must live like this. I became sullen and angry. The heaviness in my heart became such a familiar, discouraging weight that it took on the persona of a gorilla sitting on my chest. I was never going to walk so I may as well stay in bed until I died.

I had no memory of my wreck, but my family was there, and they slowly helped me piece the accident together. My mom told me that according to the police report, it looked like I had fallen asleep at the wheel, plowed through a barbed wire fence and hit a tree that split my car in half. I was thrown in the back seat, where I was pinned, but alive. I had to be cut out of the car, and it was a miracle that I had survived the accident.

From the wreck I was taken by ambulance to the small hospital in Purvis. Because of my life-threatening injuries, I was immediately transferred to the University Medical Center in

Jackson, MS. My youngest sister, Shawn, met the ambulance coming into the Emergency Room at the hospital. She could hear me yelling and then see the staff trying to control me as I battled the EMTs and hospital attendants. I was yelling and swinging my arms in pain and hysteria.

From the time I entered the University Medical Center until the time I woke up six weeks later, there was one crisis after another. My traumatic brain injury required immediate attention as my brain was swelling at an alarming rate. If pressure wasn't relieved soon, I would die from the swelling. I fell into a coma. The surgical staff drilled a hole in my skull and installed a shunt to relieve the pressure. A trachea was done and a ventilator installed. I was on the ventilator for more than six weeks. It was a long "wait and see game" for my family who did not know if I would ever wake up.

My legs were crushed in the accident. Surgeons tried to lay out a plan for putting my legs back together, but then gangrene set in. There were multiple amputations. The surgeons wanted to leave as much leg as possible but stay ahead of the gangrene. There were transfusions, and, eventually, I received a total of 52 units of blood. When I finally woke up, it was after yet another surgery, and thankfully, that was the last amputation. My left stump ended a few inches below my knee and my right stump ended mid-thigh. My stumps needed painful skin grafts which were taken from high on my thighs. These grafts added misery and pain to my healing process. There were debridement procedures that were beyond painful but had to be done.

The first two weeks after I woke up, I stayed in the recovery room. There were no beds in intensive care, but I needed intense care. So, I was kept in recovery until a bed opened up for me. A room finally opened at the terrible expense of another's life. There was a man in the ICU recovering from gunshot wounds. He was making progress when his assailant hunted him down in the hospital and shot him again. This time he died. No one knew how this aggressor got in, but he was captured before he could leave the premises. My sister, Shawn, reminded me of this interesting side note. Overall, it was a macabre story that, nevertheless, I found unexplainably funny. Someone finally had it worse than me and I got a room because of it.

While my body healed, I was depressed. My despondency turned to boiling rage that this had happened to me. I blamed God. I blamed my car. I blamed fate. I could see no positive outcome, no future. I did not see that I would ever be able to work or take care of myself or that any woman would ever want me. Everywhere I looked, I saw nothing but pain. I would have to live like an invalid and rely on other people to take care of me. Again, I decided I would rather be dead.

My New Hebron girlfriend came to visit and I froze her out. No way did I want her around to see me struggle to do all the normal things I had done before. There was one time that I had two girlfriends show up at the same time (a painful reminder of the heathen life I was living). It was bad timing all the way around. Neither girlfriend knew about the other and it was plain bad luck that they showed up at the same time. No way did I want their pity and I did not want them to see me in such pain. I was rude to both and got them out of there as fast as I could. I didn't want anyone to see me like this, not now, not ever.

I sometimes thought I was losing my mind. My mind would not or could not accept the tragedy of the crash. Pain became my everyday companion. All of the nerves that had led down my legs and feet were still alive but stopped at the bottom of my stumps. Those shortened nerves triggered continuously, and while it was called phantom pain (as though it didn't exist), it haunted my days and tortured my nights. I was pumped full of pain meds and that helped, but it didn't totally relieve the pain.

During this time, I could not think straight. Besides the pain and the weight on my chest, I could not see any future. What would it look like? How would I live or work or take care of myself? I couldn't see past the end of my stumps, and when I could, all I saw were the things I couldn't do.

Eventually, I was well enough to move from critical to stable condition and from stable to ready for rehab. The hospital staff was relentless and transferred me to their rehab unit. Every hour of every day was purposely filled with one activity after another, all aimed at getting me independent and out the front door. In the mornings, they dragged me out of bed and forced me to go to both physical and occupational therapy. My physical healing expanded a bit to include my mental healing.

I had been in a coma for more than six weeks. There were a couple of more weeks spent healing in bed. Before my accident, I weighed 185 pounds and was 5' 11-½". My weight dropped to 120 pounds. The loss of my legs accounted for the bulk of the loss, but not all. I lost most of my muscle tone and was easily exhausted.

Mom was there every day and most nights. She watched me like a hawk and kept the hospital staff on their toes. She stayed on top of my meds. Made sure I ate. Made sure the hospital staff did their job to keep me clean and comfortable, especially during the time I was in a coma. When I was awake, she would chat with me if I was up to it. She also quietly attended to my needs and her presence was comforting.

Because I was in a university hospital, there were doctor rounds every day. A team of six or seven students with a resident doctor would enter the room and circle my bed. My case would be presented to the students followed by questions and answers. They talked about me as though I were the deaf, mute and blind lab rat of the day. No one talked directly to me. The process was humiliating and to this day, it makes me angry to think about the experience.

There was concern over my mental recovery. After a six week-long coma, my mother was told I might never come out of a vegetative state. When I first woke up, I was given mental tests. There were many simple questions. I was asked for my current address and I didn't know it. Who did I work for? I couldn't remember. I knew I should know these answers, but I couldn't think of them. I knew my name. I knew my mother. But I couldn't remember my favorite food. I could not do simple arithmetic. My mother was ecstatic that I knew who she was, but I was upset that I didn't know the simplest answers. With time all those memories did return, except my actual car wreck, and family helped me know what happened while I was in a coma.

There was the daily trip to hydrotherapy. I would soak in a warm whirlpool tub. My skin grafts were wrapped in a Saran wrap looking bandage that was clear and transparent. My grafts would be carefully checked and any healing progression was noted. When it became apparent that I was healing properly, this clear bandage was ripped off, tearing my skin grafts. I bled and it was painful. Different bandaging was applied and my grafts slowly healed and physical therapy could begin.

When rehab started, I was as weak as a baby. I did not make superhuman progress, but slow and steady progress. Day by day, my arm strength returned. My core muscles returned to help me keep my balance. Every day I pushed a little harder to force my body to do more than the day before. I would need the additional arm and core strength to transfer from my wheelchair to the bed, the car, and the toilet. My appetite returned and I ate with delight.

In my head and heart, I was an athlete. My body responded to the physical challenge of rehab in an unexpected way. Therapy forced my muscles to respond in spite of my sour disposition. I got stronger. Therapy showed me how to move independently. I was taught how to transfer by myself from bed to chair. How to climb over curbs without spilling out of the chair. How to get back in a chair by myself if I did take a spill. I was taught how to cook for myself and how to balance a plate on my lap while moving around in my chair.

Walter was my physical therapist. He wore glasses, was slim and a soft spoken, gentle guy who worked me like a dog. He filled both therapy roles of physical and occupational. He was kind, but relentlessly encouraged me to go "one more." Didn't matter what I was struggling to do, he wanted "one more."

Each morning hospital staff would help me transfer from the bed to my chair which was a relatively big drop. Once I was in the chair, I wheeled myself over to Walter's venue. There the torture would begin. I did upper body strength building, lots of curls with increasing weight as I progressed. I worked a contraption called the rickshaw that I would back into and grab handles and pump. As time passed, the weight I was lifting became heavier. This machine helped me build the muscles I would need to be fully independent again.

Each day for the next several weeks was a repetition of the day before. I spent mornings with Walter who coaxed, hounded and cheered me into working harder. Then came a two-hour break for a communal lunch for all of us working in physical therapy. We would laugh and encourage each other, swap tales, and share our progress. There was unrest in the room, but I stayed away from it. The last thing I needed was to be brought any further down by whining and anger that didn't help me cope with my new life or my old anger. The afternoons were spent in the recreation room. There were lowered pool tables, foosball games, air hockey and ping pong. I played lots of pool and foosball. At 4:30 the rec room closed and my workday was complete. Then came naps, dinner, and TV.

I loved the TV in my room. It wasn't hung on the wall across the room but was close to my bed. I watched "Outlaw Dirt Track Races" and other "guy TV" half the night. When my night meds kicked in, I would drift off until the nurse's aide came to take my vitals. Twice a night they woke me up for this. I decided that the last place a sick person should be is in the hospital. You are not allowed to get a full night's sleep.

I battled my fear as I got stronger. I couldn't see my future life yet and it tormented me. I couldn't go back to construction for the power company. I couldn't see myself working at a desk. I loved being outside, even in the hot Mississippi sun and high humidity. "What am I going to do? What am I going to do?" rolled around in my head like a couple of marbles going nowhere. I hated being so dependent on everyone else for even the simplest thing even a glass of water.

Despite my attitude there was progress through the weeks. My strength began to return. Eventually I could transfer from bed to chair without help. When I could do that consistently, I got myself out of bed and wheeled myself down the hall to Walter.

When the bandages on my stumps came off, I could also go to and from the shower by myself. This was a blessing in and of itself. I felt a small measure of independence returning when I could keep myself clean. It was humiliating to be given a bed bath. I was a grown man even if I was a cripple. I still had that "cripple" mentality, and I did not yet have the strength to throw that attitude away.

God bless Walter. He introduced me to a magazine called "Sports N Spokes." I had never imagined that there would be sports where all the participants would be in wheelchairs. My idea of people in wheelchairs were invalids being pushed around because they were too feeble to push themselves. According to this magazine, even people in wheelchairs could be athletes. This was a new concept for me. It opened my mind to a new world of possibilities and with that, my attitude became more positive. With a new and different perspective my horizon began to expand.

I was still mad at myself. If I had been asked what I wanted, I would have said "kill me now." But God wasn't listening to that prayer. Eventually, I came to know in my heart that I was running from God, not just figuratively, but literally. God wanted my full attention, and I wasn't ready to give it to Him. Until I could get to that point, the weight of that gorilla stayed square on my chest.

There were outside activities that distracted me from my self-centeredness and misery. Once a week we went to the movies. This was a production in that we loaded into a handicapped van via motorized ramps and were locked into wheelchair equipped riding slots. We sat in the back aisle of the theater to watch the movie. One of the movies we saw was One Flew Over the Cuckoo's Nest. I found this an appropriate movie for the condition we were all in with plenty of morbid humor and we all hated Nurse Ratched. We went back to the rehab planning our escape.

Another time we went to a ballgame to see the minor league Jackson team play. We went once a week to a bowling alley that was set up for wheelchair bowling. We couldn't swing the ball and release it, so there was a special ramp that we could move to aim and then release the ball. Every outside activity was something to look forward to.

My phantom pain haunted me from the first moment I woke up. There wasn't any relief. It was something I would have to learn to live with. I was told that eventually the pain would subside and then go away. In the meantime, it was an almost constant companion. I could feel my toes and the arch in my foot. The cramps in the calves of my legs were real and terrible. When I looked at my aching legs and feet, nothing was there, except the pain. It was disorienting and confusing.

As my time in rehab became shorter, I received driver's training. It was like flying without any instructions, both exhilarating and terrifying at the same time. At first it was shocking to get behind the wheel and not be able to use my feet. My hands and feet had always been my connection to my car. I could feel acceleration through my feet, same thing for braking. All control was now through my left hand. I accelerated and braked with my left hand. Steered with my right hand. What had become second nature in controlling my vehicle had to be unlearned and a new way learned. My brain stubbornly could not make the new connections. It took multiple times behind the wheel before I began to make the new connection from my brain to my left hand. My progress was slow.

We drove around the medical center. Around and around, until I began to feel comfortable. My trainer was soft spoken and patient. When he felt I was making headway, we began to drive on city streets. Slowly the fear subsided. Braking began to feel safer. Acceleration felt more normal. I began to feel more in control behind the wheel. I was not comfortable, but I could see my own progress, and I began to see that I could live independently after all.

Then, there were times when I was flooded with memories. They came unbidden and haunted me in a way that I could not escape. I was overwhelmed with all the things I would never do again...

8

The Bicycle Ride

After college and before my first job I planned a bicycle ride with a cycling buddy from Jackson, Mississippi. The total route was approximately 850 miles so this was not going to be a short trip, but an epic adventure. I bought a Schwinn 21-speed Super Le Tour chromed bike with special racks for panniers to carry camping equipment and extra clothes. I switched my daily running routine to the bike and rode whenever possible. On weekends I'd ride up to thirty miles a day. This was far from sufficient, but I told myself that as a runner, this was plenty of training for the ride. One of my shortcomings in this training is that I only trained with the weight of my body. Hopping on that bike with another 45 pounds of gear would be a rude awakening that would slow me down and make me ache the first few hundred miles of the trip.

The planned route for this trip would start on the Natchez Trace Parkway in Madison, Mississippi. The Natchez Trace is an old trading route from Natchez to Nashville, Tennessee. This two-lane National Scenic Parkway is 444 miles long and is managed by the National Park Service. Since we would be starting in Madison, we would not be riding the entire trace, only a part of it. From Nashville the plan was to head to Mammoth Cave National Park in Kentucky.

From Mammoth Cave, my plan was to travel to the Smoky Mountain National Park and then connect to the Blue Ridge Parkway which begins in the U.S. 250/Skyline Drive town of Rockfish Gap, Virginia on the North end. 469 miles to the South at U.S. 441 in Swain County, North Carolina is where I would start. It was a challenging route, and I hoped to squeeze in a side trip to Washington, DC before catching a bus home.

My buddy Paul would be riding the first leg of the journey with me. Paul was a pre-med student who had to return to school in Jackson after we reached Mammoth Cave. We started out in mid-summer and kept up a solid pace so that Paul could make his school deadline. We rode hard every day without stopping to sightsee. We each carried a tent and a sleeping bag. Freeze dried meals kept us going and health bars kept us traveling between meals. We made camp whenever we had enough of the road for the day.

Paul was amiable company and we would commiserate over the fact that neither of us were in great shape for such a long ride. One of my knees ached all the way through Mississippi, but mysteriously stopped when we crossed into Alabama. Paul had his own aches and pains. Some days the rides were easy and downhill, and some days it seemed like the entire day was spent pedaling uphill.

During one stretch Paul and I came to a "Road Closed" sign and decided that was the way to go. Eventually the paved road turned into a dirt road and ended with an uncompleted bridge. We waded through the stream below and held our bicycles and all our gear over our heads. The cool, refreshing water reached our waistlines by midstream, but we came out the other side without mishap and with dry gear. The next bridge was more complete. We balanced our bikes overhead again, but this time we were able to carefully walk across.

At our campfire that night we could hear the frogs and watch the lightning bugs. We fell into easy conversation and shared the truth of Jesus and eternal life. In the beauty of nature and away from the complications of life, it is easy to feel close to God. I "talked the talk," but I still wasn't "walking the walk." Even so, taking that closed road was one of the memorable events of the journey.

Eventually, our side trip led back to the main route and the journey continued. We rode into Mammoth Cave National Park and ended the first leg of this journey. Paul and I had ridden together for over 400 miles.

I had a new girlfriend named Libby, who was interning at Mammoth Cave National Park. Paul and I both crashed at Libby's that first night. It was raining the next day when we dropped Paul off at the bus station where he was headed to Jackson and school.

From Mammoth Cave National Park, I had about a 270-mile ride southeast to the Great Smoky Mountains. I found that riding alone had some great advantages. I stopped to rest when I felt like it. Traveled at my own pace. Ate when my stomach demanded it. Stopped to camp when and where I chose. I could stop to sightsee or travel. Some days I covered 20 miles, some days, when I felt like a cycling machine, more than 100.

I made it to the Smoky Mountain National Park where I cycled to a height of 6,644 feet to reach Clingman's Dome. I was worried that 21 gears on my bike wouldn't be enough, but I did make it. My legs were screaming at me and I was exhausted but happy with my performance.

At the top of the mountain, there was an observation tower with a sweeping 375-foot-long ramp for visitors to reach the tower. I parked my bike and with trembling legs walked to the tower that was 45 feet off the ground. I sat and took in the spectacular 360-degree view of mountains, trees and sparkling blue sky. Eventually my legs returned to normal and I made my way down the ramp to my locked bike.

In the parking lot, I met a fellow cyclist named David. He was from Washington State and had already ridden across most of America. He had plans to ride to the East coast, ending his ride somewhere in Virginia. We made plans to ride together for a while. He hiked up to the dome and I waited at the base for his return. My legs were still a little wobbly and just sitting felt great.

The weather turned into chilly rain, so David and I looked around for a place to camp. Instead, we found a nice dry bathroom at the base of Clingman's Dome and dragged our bicycles and gear inside. It was still cold, but at least it was dry. About an hour later, four backpackers that were hiking the Appalachian Trail stumbled in wet and exhausted. All six of us settled in for the night. It was cramped, six of us trying to stretch out enough to sleep with bicycles and backpacks stacked everywhere.

Sometime that night while it was storming with thunder and lightning, a Park Ranger stopped and did a flashlight inspection. It probably wasn't the first time he had found campers stuffed in a bathroom, and we were delighted when he only looked around and left. We drifted back to sleep, each one of us happy that we didn't get kicked out and had been allowed to sleep on the floor of a public park bathroom.

The next morning, the hikers continued on and David and I hit the road together. This was a short-lived double ride. We stopped at an overlook sometime the next morning and a couple in an RV pulled up beside us. David persuaded the couple to let him hitch a ride with them. Off he went grinning and waving from the back window of the camper.

I don't know why this made me so mad, but it did. I think I was jealous that he got a ride and took it. Even though I had enjoyed my ride alone, I was also looking forward to having someone to travel with and talk to. Now, here I was all alone again. I still had several hundred miles to go and the thought of forcing myself to finish was losing its appeal fast.

I resigned myself to traveling alone and headed out once again. At least the rain had stopped. The sun was peeking through the clouds here and there. I had only gone a few miles when the traffic in both directions came to a dead stop. Slowly the traffic inched forward and ahead I could see a momma bear and her cub ambling along the edge of the road. In the park wildlife roams free and has the right of way. Traffic was carefully and very slowly moving around the two bears.

Getting around the bears was tough for me. My side of the traffic was uphill and it was extremely difficult to get any momentum on the steep incline. I was impatient and angry, and while others were enjoying momma bear and her cub, I missed the fun of the scenery and stewed in my juices. Eventually, I got around them and made it to the Blue Ridge Parkway.

The Blue Ridge had a 45 MPH speed limit, which didn't mean much to a lone cyclist. The Parkway was a roller coaster ride of startling elevation changes and no guardrails. While traveling uphill was a test of guts and leg endurance, rolling downhill was often exhilarating and terrifying at the same time. One wrong twitch on the handlebars and I could be thrown off the road into the forested abyss.

One of my memorable stops on the Blue Ridge Parkway wasn't a view or meeting new people. It was an open restaurant and I was starving. After three weeks on the road, I was sick of dehydrated meals and snack bars and I craved real food. I ordered a meal and gobbled it down. I was still hungry, so I ordered a different meal, and likewise, I gobbled it down, too. I was shocked that I was still hungry and ordered yet another meal. I ate every bite and finally, I was full and satisfied. Three full dinners topped my calorie tank and I was now recovered. A short nap, and I was ready to go again.

I decided on a stop in Asheville, NC. My wheels needed truing and I hadn't learned to do that for myself yet. My bicycle was a standard factory-issue bike and I hadn't made any adjustments for the extra weight of my gear or for the long tour I was on. The wheels were beginning to wobble ever so slightly so it was time for maintenance. I was still in the mountains, fighting the inclines up and holding my breath on the down slopes. At a scenic rest stop I met a driver who let me know he had clocked me at 50 MPH going down one of the recent hills. I didn't have a speedometer on the bike, and while I knew I was going at a good, fast clip, I had no idea just how fast I was going. I decided I better slow it down a bit until I had the work done on my bike.

As I headed into Asheville, my back tire blew-out. When I stopped, I found a 2-inch tear in the tire and that my inner tube had exploded. At first, I was so mad, I couldn't see the blessing. All I could see was that I would have to push my bike all the way into town. It took a while to realize just how lucky I had been. If my tire had exploded while I was racing 50 MPH down that wooded highway mountain road with no guard rails, I would have gone over the edge. Nobody would have found my body, maybe ever. The animals would have had a feast.

My good luck continued as I pushed my disabled bike into Asheville and one of the first businesses, I came to be a bike shop. The owner was cordial, but insisted he could not get to my bike until Monday. Then I realized it was only Friday and that I would be forced to campout for three days. I was overwhelmed and angry at the delay. As I left the shop, trying to decide what I would do for the next three days, I looked up and saw a Trailways bus station directly ahead. I decided then and there to end my ride, catch a bus home and be done with my adventure.

I returned to the bike shop and the owner gave me a bicycle shipping box. I had enough money in traveler's checks to buy a ticket for me and to ship my bike home. I didn't pray about ending my journey home, as I have said, I gave God some lip service, but he wasn't running my show, yet.

As I climbed on the bus for the ride home, I felt like a failure. I had planned an 836-mile adventure and had only made it 580 miles. At first this qualified as a total failure, I did not reach my final destination of Washington, D.C., but there was a lot more to my trip than that. During the twenty-hour ride home, I gave myself over to contemplating all the wonderful things that had happened along the way.

The detour on the closed road that Paul and I had taken was filled with delightful challenges. We had crossed the stream with bikes overhead and felt like jungle warriors. Crossing the partial bridge balancing on the beams and using our bikes as counterbalances made us feel unstoppable. I loved the time we spent around the campfire talking about Jesus, when I so desperately needed him, but was stubbornly unwilling to let him in.

While I was at Mammoth Cave Park, I found a waterfall with a small cavern behind it. I had to navigate a narrow and dark path to get to the cavern, but once there, the feeling was magical.

The falling sheet of water gave the forest beyond it a shimmering mysterious aura. I felt a sweet safe peace and decided to camp there for the night. The cavern was deep enough for me to stay dry. The soft rush of the waterfall lulled me to sleep and I awoke the next morning charged and refreshed, ready to meet the challenges of the bike ride ahead.

After leaving Mammoth Cave National Park, I was headed to the Smoky Mountain National Park. Along the way I went through Franklin, Kentucky and stopped for a memorable day.

Outside of a convenience store I met the current state Moto-Cross champion and we had a short chat. Both of us were passionate about what we were doing, and we clicked. I have remembered the conversation for close to forty years, even though I can't for the life of me remember his name.

I toured a fish hatchery and was amazed at the size and quantity of separate tanks. Fish of all varieties were grown for state lakes and for private property owners to stock their ponds. I had a short, guided tour and was left to explore on my own. I was interested in the process of hatchlings to ready-for-market fish. After a couple of hours, I moved on.

I attended my first Bluegrass festival and my rock and roll soul moved over to allow this special music in. It was a great place to "people watch." There were families with little kids hopping up and down in rhythm to the music. Old folks were tapping their toes and smiling. Young people were chasing each other and howling in laughter. People everywhere were fanning themselves and eating cold slices of watermelon. The performers were a plentiful variety of people wearing fancy matching outfits to those wearing simple overalls and t-shirts. One thing they all had in common was a heartfelt devotion to the music that extended out to draw the entire audience in. I was surprised at how much I enjoyed this new music and spent the afternoon listening to songs that sang of Jesus.

The next morning, I headed east toward the Smoky Mountains. I had a long way to go, but the inner glow of the day before was still with me. I passed a giant field-spider web that made me stop and look again. The web was huge and covered several lines of barbed wire. It was covered in dew drops that sparkled like diamonds in the early morning sunlight. I drank the sight in and left the spider in one piece, even though if I had found that giant in my yard, I would have squashed him immediately. But, not this morning, I felt awe in the splendor of God's creation.

As I sat on the bus, I remembered the stranded lady who had a flat tire in the middle of nowhere. She didn't have a clue how to change a tire and was in total despair. I stopped to help and she immediately brightened in appreciation. We chatted amiably as I changed her tire. She was grateful for my help and I was pleased with myself for doing the right thing. There were many of these memories on this ride.

So, no, I had not made the total trip, but I had gone 580 miles. There weren't many people who had taken such a long ride, camped out and enjoyed all the sights I had. I decided to call this trip a complete success, even if I hadn't gone the total distance.

These memories were so bittersweet to me. I would revel through them with tears, regret and utter longing. I would never again make a trip like this, but God had plans to give me something else that was even better. I just couldn't see it at the time.

9

And Finally, God

Right before Christmas, almost four months after my wreck, rehab released me. I moved home with WG and my mother. This is not what I wanted to do. After all the years of trying to get away from WG, here I was dependent upon him again. Mom was great, as always, but I was depressed and bored. I wanted my old life back and I brooded on it, trying to accept that I would never live that way again. I will say that Mom's great cooking helped me gain back the weight I had lost.

One afternoon while sitting around bored again, I remembered Eddie, the Campus Life leader who had led me to the Lord in high school. We had stayed in touch over the years, but only in a casual way. I had never shared any of the details of my wild living with him. Now, I looked him up and gave him a call that turned out to be a "divine appointment" that God used as a step in my healing.

Our conversation began with vague day-to-day catching up. Eddie was congenial and I shared with him the details of losing my legs. I told him I was recovering and doing fine, but that I had not yet gone back to work. I was still talking when in the background, I could hear Eddie softly weeping. What? This man that had led me to the Lord was now crying for me. I had never seen or heard anyone cry for me over the loss of my legs, not even Mom. Yet, this dear brother in Christ living several hundred miles away in another state was crying for me.

And now, I was weeping for all the pain and the loss and my own feelings of hopelessness. This one phone call pulled up my pain from deep within. Out came my bad decisions, missed opportunities, and my willful and deliberate disobedience to God. In came the peace of God through the soft, encouraging words of my old friend. Eddie told me that everything would be okay, and I felt relief at the words even if I wasn't sure I believed him. He suggested that I get a copy of the book "Joni" and read it. He promised it would help me adjust to my situation. When I hung up the phone, I felt exhausted, but oddly refreshed and hopeful about my future for the first time.

I took Eddie's advice and ran down a copy of "Joni." This is the story of a competitive high school diver who dove into a shallow spot in the lake and broke her neck. The accident left her a quadriplegic. Joni struggles with her disability. She is confident that if the correct God-anointed people pray for her, she will be healed and restored to full health. It doesn't happen, but Joni isn't discouraged. In fact, she continues to trust in God and encourage others. She quoted a couple of Biblical verses that had a profound effect on me:

> And He said to me, "My grace is sufficient for you, for My strength is made perfect in weakness." 2 Cor. 12:9 NKJV

I read this scripture. I read it again. I read it a third time and it was like the Lord himself wrapped his arms around me. In my head and in my heart I knew God had forgiven me for all my wicked living and all of my wrong turns. I knew my life had to change. I knew that God had a purpose for me, but I would have to seek after him. He literally touched me that day, mentally, physically and spiritually. My lost desire to live was restored with this one verse.

> "And we know all things work together for good to them that love God, to them who are called according to his purpose."
>
> Rom. 8:28 NKJV

After reading this scripture, I immediately yelled to God, "What good can come from this?" In typical two steps forward, one step back healing, I was still hurting, still doubting, still asking questions. I was still in a state of confusion and shaking my Bible at God in anger. Looking back to that uncertain time in my life, I can now see how God came alongside me to guide me and lead me in the direction that He had planned for my life. His words, His plan. I was no longer the master of my own destiny, God was. He would be the key that unlocked my future.

One afternoon while I was feeling despondent, Mom saw that I was down and struggling. She suggested, "Why don't you go down to our neighbor's pool and dangle your feet in the water."

I couldn't believe my ears, "What did you say?"

She repeated, "Go to the neighbors and dangle your feet in the pool."

"Mom" I yelled at her, "I don't have any feet!"

In that instant, the absurdity of what she'd said sank in. She collapsed on the floor in hysterical laughter and I joined her. We laughed until we were both crying. As the tears rolled down both of our faces, reality and healing seeped into my heart. If I could laugh at my own disaster then maybe it wasn't such a disaster after all.

I had prayed many times to have God restore my legs. For a long time, that had been my daily prayer. But now, I was beginning to see that God would walk with me and for me for the rest of my life. God wrapped his arms around me and showed me that I would never be alone. He assured me that I was of value to Him. No legs, incapacitated, and wheelchair bound, I still had great value to Him. "His strength made perfect in my weakness" showed me that I was not supposed to live without His help. But God, being full of love, mercy and grace restored a future that I had trouble seeing. The joy of being alive was restored, to live and breathe, to interact with people and live life to its fullest. God touched me physically, mentally, spiritually, and personally.

As I continued my physical rehabilitation, I found myself fascinated with competitive wheelchair racing. I would have to get in shape for it. I would need a different kind of wheelchair than my Everest & Jennings folding wheelchair. It would also give me a connection to other people in the area who were trying to adjust to their new lives without workable legs.

I became my own trainer/coach. My training course was the rural roads in Terry, MS where I was living with my folks. I attached a bright orange triangle flag to my wheelchair so that the country drivers wouldn't run me down. I added 15 pounds of weight to my chair to increase resistance. I wore leather work gloves to protect my hands from overuse and braking. While my chair did have brakes on both sides, they were for locking my chair so I wouldn't roll around. They were never meant to be used like brakes on a car to slow down and stop. Braking while in the chair meant using my hands to cause resistance and gradually slow the chair down.

My style and form were a learning experience, I had no technique. I had to learn how much force to use on the push-rims and how to grip those rims while working out. I worked myself up to a mile or two in that chair. Then, one day, while flying downhill faster than I could push, I had an adrenaline-pumping mishap that convinced me I needed a racing wheelchair. I didn't turn over. I didn't hurt myself. I was totally, terrifyingly flying down a steep hill with wheels wobbling out of control. When I was finally able to get control of my chair, and the panic in my chest settled down, I decided the chair I was in had to be replaced.

I had scared myself into spending some of my hard-earned savings on a better piece of equipment. A top-of-the-line racing wheelchair could cost several thousand dollars, which I did not have. Performance, balanced against the financial constraints of my savings account, guided my hunt for the best compromise I could find. The chair I eventually bought was all aluminum and completely adjustable. When it came in, it was a challenge to get it together and adjusted to my body. But I persevered through the frustrations of that experience and ended up with a chair that was made for speed and fit my body perfectly. Once my orange flag was in place, I was ready to train in earnest.

One of my first surprises was on my maiden run. After pushing to the top of a hill, I found I could allow all the speed on the downward slope to go into the wheels. I was in complete control, no teetering from the wheels as the speed increased, and the joy of going full tilt down the hill washed through me. There was no need to grab at the wheels to slow the chair down. Exhilaration pumped through me as I came to the bottom of the hill and again began to push to maintain that fierce speed. The more I pushed, the more my blood pumped. I grinned and pumped and pushed for more response from my body. There came a familiar sensation, a runner's high, and my elation took another jump forward as I continued to push as hard as I could for as long as I could. My brain had accepted that I would never again experience a runner's high, but that was a lie from hell.

At the end of that wild ride, I was pushing my chair up the rough gravel driveway to my parent's house. I stopped in complete exhaustion and marveled at the feelings running through my body. I felt exactly the way I used to feel when I finished my five-mile runs. It was the same euphoria, even while winded and with my heart pounding in my chest, I felt great. Tears of joy flowed down my face that I could not stop. At that moment, I cried out to God in thanksgiving. I thanked Him for what He had done, for changing my life, and for giving me hope again.

It took some time to understand what had happened. I had no legs. I could not bike. I could not walk. I could not run. That was my focus. But God gave me back all those runner's high feelings. There was another way to live, and God would take me there. I thanked God for this blessing. It was the turning point in my mental restoration as I quit looking back at my limitations and turned to this sweet new promise of a future that God was showing me.

I joined the Mississippi Track Club which promoted running events in the Jackson area. At that time, there were only able-bodied runners in their organization. I was an oddity that could not keep up with any of them for long. That would change over the years as my body responded to hard workouts and I got faster. Eventually none of them would be able to keep up with me. I moved from that weird guy in the wheelchair to a respected and admired member of their team. They would later add their own wheelchair division. But it certainly did not start out that way.

In early spring of 1983, I entered my first competitive road race, the Blue Cross Blue Shield 10K. There were no other wheelchair racers, only me. While everyone was crowded around me shoulder to shoulder, I sat shoulder to knee with everyone else. I was surrounded by legs that I could not see through or around. I couldn't see the course ahead of me for the legs in front of me. I struggled for position on the city streets only to realize that I was surrounded by competitors juggling to get around me and ahead of me. I had to be careful not to cross in front of anyone or to let anyone trip over me. If I spilled out of my chair, I would get trampled. Runners passed me left and right, but I kept plugging. Eventually, there was only one runner behind me.

There were 60-70 runners entered in this race and I finished 30 seconds ahead of the last place finisher. My time was 38:44 for the 10K run, pitiful, really. The surprise for me was that I was thrilled to cross the finish line and I was amazed at the enthusiastic applause from the crowd. Everywhere people were smiling at me and clapping me on the back as though I had won first place. I was hooked!

I played on a basketball team for a while. This was a crazy endeavor that didn't last a full year. It was chaos on the court. Players jockeyed for position and ran into or through anyone in their way. It was a demolition derby in wheelchairs. I could not protect one of my stumps from the chaos and pain of the other players running into me to get the ball. I found I much preferred competitions where all the players were going in the same direction.

One year I was invited to become a member of the United States Amputee Athletic Team going to Sudbury, Canada. Six of us went as a team. We traveled in an old motorhome and our coach stacked all six of our chairs on top of the vehicle so there would be enough room for us inside. I competed in the shot put because that was one of my events in high school. I also participated in an individual race and a team relay. I enjoyed the camaraderie but didn't care to race in circles around a track.

I placed in shot put and one of the racing events, but ended up in the hospital with a kidney stone. Now, thirty-five years later, I can't remember which event I missed. I just remember that the kidney stone took all the fun out of going to Canada and is the one thing that I do clearly remember about that trip.

10

Thriving, but Challenged

A full year after my car wreck I went back to work for the same construction company. I couldn't do my old job, but my company found a place for me in their maintenance department. I ordered parts, expedited delivery, and helped maintain the inventory. This was in the days before computers, so all this inventory management was tediously done on a handwritten Kardex file.

I was happy to have productive work, but there were adjustments I had to make to do the job. Inconvenience #1 - I was confined indoors, and some days the walls seemed to close in on me. Inconvenience #2 - Most of my co-workers were well-meaning and wanted to help but got in the way. There were also a few souls who were not so well-meaning and would grab the handles on the back of my chair and run me every which way thinking that they were hilarious while they rammed me into corners and other furniture. They would tilt me backward so that I was totally out of control and he- haw at their own antics. After that I cut the handles off of every chair, I sat in so that I could stay in control of my wheelchair and body. To this day, I will not ride in a chair with back handles. If I need help, I will ask for it. Inconvenience #3 - I did not ask for, nor want, anyone's pity, but it seemed to be on every face and I hated to see co-workers looking at me and whispering. Inconvenience #4 - Not all my pathways were easy to navigate in a chair. I had to learn how to get around tight spots in a work environment. Eventually, God helped me work out all these problems and I settled in to do my job.

I bought a 1982 Silver Buick Riviera with a white vinyl roof. The car was loaded. It had a sunroof, all electric options, and a light gray cloth interior. This was an upgrade to comfort for me. I could collapse my wheelchair and swing it behind the driver's seat. My car was fitted with hand controls and my freedom expanded, but driving was not always smooth sailing.

One rainy muggy afternoon I was out in my car, destination long forgotten. The road was hilly, up, and down like a roller coaster. I was enjoying the quiet ride of the Riviera, the patter of rain on the roof and the purring of the air conditioner. As I was approaching the crest of a hill, a driver in a pick-up truck topped the hill and was half-way in my lane. As he bearded directly down on me, I panicked. He swerved into his lane and I swerved toward the ditch in my lane. All at once my car was spinning out of control. I held on for dear life as my car hydroplaned two complete 360 degree turns. I was not braking or giving gas. I was free spinning. The pick-up passed me on the left and then I braked, coming to a full stop perpendicular to the road and taking up both lanes. This happened in an instant. I slowly gathered my senses and looked both ways, there was not a car in sight. I realized God's hand was once again upon me and He had saved me from yet another car wreck. Thankfulness overwhelmed me. It was still gently raining as I turned the wheels of my undamaged car and headed to wherever I was going. Every time I thought of that near-miss, I was overwhelmed with gratitude.

I rented a small one bedroom, one bath apartment. It was wheelchair accessible, and while it wasn't too fancy, it was my own. I happily moved in and for the first time since my accident, I was truly independent.

The joy that my independence brought me, led me right back to Christ and I picked up my Bible with enthusiasm. Again and again, I would read,

> "My grace is sufficient for you, for My strength is made perfect in weakness." 2 Cor. 12-9 NKJV

For me there were many encounters with Christ in the years after losing my legs. I do not have the ability to explain these touches from God. I only know that my life took on more meaning and I could see that I had a future. I was NOT a cripple in a wheelchair, but a solid man of God. I was no longer 5'11-½" tall, but I was still a complete man, shorter, but complete nevertheless. I was strong and athletic. I could take care of myself without any help from anyone, and as long as I "walked" with God, I would have a future.

From the time I was in my early twenties I have had the occasional kidney stone. Some of them passed with relative ease and some required hospital time. Sometime during 1983, I was in the hospital with yet another kidney stone. There must have been a shortage of beds, as I was given a room on the pediatric floor. A pretty young brunette with short hair and big brown eyes caught my attention. She had a beautiful hour-glass shape, and she was a refreshing change from the other nurses I had met since losing my legs. Her name was Betty and I found myself smiling every time she entered my room.

Betty was kind, with an easy laugh, and I found myself flirting outrageously with her every time she passed my room. When I was dismissed from the hospital, she invited me to supper at her house. I was delighted to have a first date since my accident and a date with a lovely beauty who was interested in me enough to ask me out.

We dated several months and I asked Betty to marry me. She said yes.

Our marriage ceremony was scheduled for an early fall afternoon. On that morning, I competed in a 5K race. I may have wanted to get married, but I was still a hard-core racer. I wasn't late to the wedding and the race settled my jittery nerves.

For some reason that I cannot fathom, I asked WG to be my best man and he happily accepted. Our relationship was so bad, I don't know what I was thinking. I was angry at him for a lifetime of hurt and humiliation. I felt I owed him for all the money he had spent on me over the years. I could not at this time reconcile my feelings and my actions. My relationship with my stepdad was an issue that would crop up again and again in our marriage.

After the wedding I moved into Betty's apartment for a short time. We then bought a ranch-style house, 2 bedroom, 1-1/2 bath. The bathrooms were not wheelchair accessible, but I worked around that. We settled in with nothing more than a few little adjustment squabbles.

We were both working and life together was pleasant with one exception, WG. We had plenty of money. Betty was a registered nurse and I was working at my old company behind a desk. We pretty much did whatever we wanted. If a fancy restaurant was where we wanted to eat, we did. If one of us was short on cash, the other one had just been paid. It was an easy going romantic start to our marriage, and I was very happy.

Several months later, Betty got pregnant and Nicholas was born on October 4, 1985. Betty had wanted to go the natural birth way, but while in delivery, every time she had a contraction, Nicholas went into fetal distress. The doctor decided that a C-Section would be much safer for our baby. I was kicked out of the delivery room and had to wait with all the other expectant fathers down the hall.

While I waited with the other soon-to-be dads, it occurred to me that I was not exactly ready to be a father. My own upbringing had not prepared me to know the correct way to raise a healthy stable child. I was fearfully apprehensive at the prospect of this unknown territory. I was also afraid that the baby might be damaged in the delivery, but not so. Nicholas came out just fine. I would have to learn on the job about becoming a good father.

At home Nicholas was top priority to both of us. Whatever the baby needed or wanted, we did our best to provide. Betty nursed and I did supplemental bottle feedings. She went back to work when her six weeks maternity leave was over and she worked from 7 PM to 3 AM. I took care of Nicholas while she worked and she watched him while I worked.

The evenings with Nick were a great bonding time. I fed him, bathed him and cuddled with him. I changed hundreds of dirty diapers and learned that it didn't kill me to change poopy diapers. When he fell asleep, I would tuck him in his crib. He was an active baby, turned over early and from then on, he was on the go. He became my little buddy and I learned how to be a dad.

God blessed me with Nick. He was an easy, smiling baby, with little or no colic. He slept well. He didn't play around with his food. It may have ended up all over his face, but he was intent on getting the macaroni and cheese or the chicken nuggets in his mouth. He laughed early and often and brought me great joy.

As he got older, we had outings. He would sit between my stumps and I would push the two of us around. He liked riding that way and I could easily contain him. We played ball, shoving it back and forth across the room while Nick laughed in glee. We watched Teenage Mutant Ninja Turtles tapes over and over on VCR. The tape would end and he immediately wanted to watch it again. So, we would watch it again. He loved to put puzzles together, so we often did that at the dining room table. He easily learned that the outside edges were important and we would race each other to grab all those flat pieces first. I read a story to him every night at bedtime before tucking him in with hugs and kisses. He seemed to grow in front of my eyes.

Betty worked every other weekend, so with that restriction, we went to church every other week at Forest Hill Baptist Church. After Nick was born, we'd drop him off at the nursery and later he went to the toddler group. From the beginning, Nick was part of a church-going family. Unfortunately, Betty and I never learned to pray together, never went to Sunday School together. I took Nick to church when Betty was working.

Our marriage began to fray around the edges, and at first, it was hard to tell any difference. There was no yelling or screaming, but things were coming apart. WG always seemed to be at the root of our disagreements. We would go visit Mom and Dad and take Nick with us. Occasionally, we would eat, but my parents were still drinking, so we never lingered for long and they never babysat for us. After a visit with my folks, Betty and I felt stressed and edgy. If we argued about anything, it was because Betty thought I was a different person when I was around my parents.

She was right, I was always different around WG. My attitude of fear and withdrawal around him had been with me since the day WG dumped the bucket of crawdads on me. I hadn't been much older than Nick when this had happened. I never did get over it, and, no, I could not boldly stand up to him every time he rudely pushed his way into our business. This drove Betty nuts and increased my resentment and anger.

One afternoon months later, WG came to our house, supposedly to talk to Betty about something she had or hadn't done. He was drunk. That time I did have the backbone to tell him he couldn't come in. That infuriated him and he began to stomp and cuss and order me to get Betty out in the yard so he could set her straight. I still wouldn't let him in and I wasn't about to send my wife out in the yard where he could hit her like he hit my mother. Eventually, he stomped off to his truck, gunned the engine to life and burned rubber halfway down the block. Betty and I did not discuss this incident, but there was a growing wall of silence between us.

Then, out of the blue Betty asked for a divorce. We hadn't been talking much, but we weren't fighting. I was stunned and thought she might change her mind. But no, she did not. Betty filed for divorce. She had the divorce papers served to me at work and that was humiliating. Even though she had told me she wanted a divorce and had seen a lawyer, I didn't believe she would go through with it. I was forced to move out and leave my family behind.

For a long time, I blamed WG for ruining my marriage to Betty, but looking back, I didn't help the situation much. I was mad at WG all the time. I did not respect him as a man or as a father, and I always felt like I owed him something. I resented feeling that way. He drank. He hit my mother. But I had plenty of shortcomings myself. I was not the spiritual head of my household as I should have been. I may have read my Bible, but I didn't share it with my wife or lead her in any way. I took her to church, but only when she wasn't working. And, when I was angry at WG, I was angry and withdrawn at home. She unfairly had to live with my anger that spilled out and over everyone I loved.

In an effort to cope, I continued working out and racing. It gave my body a chance to work off the anger and disappointment that plagued me. I missed my son and seeing him every other weekend was a far cry from living at home with him. I missed my wife but the wall that I had put up was set in concrete and there was no overcoming that. I resented the separation and when she moved to another state and took Nick with her, I was devastated. My attorney at the time said there was nothing I could do about it. So, every other weekend turned into never for more than two years until she moved back.

Without racing, my life would have been totally out of control. I stayed in racing shape and took every opportunity I could to compete. My personal 10K best time was 28:10 at the Peachtree Road Race in Atlanta, Georgia. I moved to 26-mile marathons. They were more challenging and I was ready to test myself at longer distances.

Wheelchairs were now a part of every marathon with their own separate start times. Wheelchairs were faster than runners, so we had an earlier start time. I had hopes of competing at the Boston Marathon, but my best time of 2:25:06 was five full minutes too slow for me to qualify. It didn't matter, I liked the challenge and eventually I could outrun all my able-bodied teammates in the Mississippi Track Club, and that was good enough for me. I raced in a total of 7 marathons. No matter what was going on in my life, I found time to participate and it helped keep me grounded and sane.

One afternoon I watched an Iron Man Triathlon on television. This is a three-part race: swimming, bicycling and running. I decided that this would be a good event for me to enter, another test of my endurance and determination. I entered a triathlon (not an ironman, which is much longer) held at the Ross Barnett Reservoir in Madison, MS and started training after work and on weekends.

Without my legs, I wasn't a very strong swimmer. My stumps were almost useless in the water as their weight made my body hang vertically. I trained at the YMCA three times a week, swimming two miles each workout. The "Y" had swimming buoys that kept my stumps in a good upward position. My arm strokes became long and competitive, while my stumps hindered me less. I checked the rules for the swimming portion of the triathlon and found there was no stipulation against using these buoys, so I bought a set for myself.

I already had a racing wheelchair for the running leg. For the bicycling leg of the race, I needed to purchase an arm-powered tricycle. I found the trike I needed from a manufacturer in California for about $1,000. WG got on the phone and nagged the manufacturer into shipping my bike ASAP, or it probably would not have arrived in time for the race. Looking back again, WG helped me lots of times when he didn't have to. The manufacturer was so new that he shipped me his prototype because he hadn't started production. It has taken writing this book for me to see just how many times WG contributed to making my life easier, either with his business savvy or his money. It is a terrible shame that he was such a jerk when he was drunk, and that he was drunk so much of the time.

When my trike came in, I found that the arm mechanism was poorly conceived. The wheels cranked like a regular bicycle, left arm, right arm, working my body doubly hard. It wasn't perfect, but it would work for this race. I had about a month to train on this new equipment before the race and though I worked my distance up quickly, I felt inadequately trained on race day. I was also the only wheelchair competitor in this triathlon.

My first triathlon was a ¼ mile swim, a 12-mile bicycle race and a 5K run. My gear went in the back of a pickup truck. I had no crew to help get my equipment to the staging area for each leg of the journey. I pushed my bike to that staging area while sitting in my chair. It was shove the bike and then push my chair, shove, then push. It was as awkward as it sounds, but I was totally determined to do this alone, whatever it took. Next, the buoys went in my lap and I wheeled as close to the water as possible for the swimming leg of the race. I scooted the remaining distance on my hands and butt to the water's edge and then swam to what I thought would be a good starting position.

The race started with all swimmers treading water and spaced out as close t0 the starting line as possible. When the horn blew every swimmer thrust mightily into the chaos. The swim leg of the triathlon was an exercise in staying alive and not getting kicked in the face. The buoys did their job and kept my stumps horizontal, but there were so many swimmers that every forward arm thrust was met with the kicking feet of the swimmer ahead of me. I couldn't swim strongly enough to get ahead of them and slowing down meant the swimmers behind me were trying to swim over me. The water was a churning bathtub making it impossible to get a full breath of air without taking in water. I was thankful this leg of the race was short, and I lagged behind in spite of my training. I wasn't the last one out of the water and that encouraged me.

A bystander met me with my wheelchair as I came out of the water. I quickly settled into my chair and with arms aching, I pushed myself to the top of the hill to retrieve my bicycle. After the swim, the bike continued to drag on my arms with the left and right pumping action, but I made it through the twelve mile bike race. I fell farther behind. For later races I would change the gearing on my bicycle so that I was pushing in the same direction with both arms as when I was in my chair. This lowered the back and forth stress on my body and greatly increased my efficiency and speed, but for today it would be left arm, right arm for all twelve miles.

The last part of the race was in my racing chair, and I excelled. The other racers' legs were becoming leaden. They plodded ahead getting heavier and slower. My chair allowed my arms to push in unison and my endurance training pumped new vigor into my arms. In my chair I was able to compete and move ahead of other competitors who had flown past me in the earlier two legs of the race. My pace was rhythmic and fast. Every time I passed a runner, I felt encouraged to pass the next runner ahead of me. I didn't win this triathlon, but I finished with a respectable time and looked forward to the next race. Just like the first time I raced in a 10K race, there was applause, handshakes and enthusiastic congratulations at the finish line.

Over my 12-year racing career, the individual races have become a blur. I enjoyed every single one of them, even if I felt like upchucking at the end of the tough ones. There were races when special things happened, and those I do remember. My first 10K, my first marathon, and my first triathlon were all special. There were other events that were special for other reasons.

There was a bicycle fundraiser across Mississippi for multiple sclerosis (MS). It was a two-day event that began in Meridian and ended in Vicksburg. The ride was 133 miles long. I hit the first hill before I left Meridian and it was a challenge. I ended up at the back of the pack, and there I stayed all day. It was a long day and my arms were heavy from fatigue by the time I pulled into our overnight stop in Roosevelt State Park in Morton. I was proud because I stuck it out, but upset that I hadn't finished with a better time. What started out as a rather discouraging day ended as a memorable night for me. Dinner was carb packed and delicious. I ate like I hadn't seen food in a week. There was an unlimited dessert table and I ate until I couldn't swallow another bite. There was the usual chatting and camaraderie after dinner when the entire support crew and all of the riders gave me a standing ovation. I had finished last for the day, but I had finished. I was embarrassed and humbled by such open admiration and encouragement. I wasn't looking for approval, but the acceptance was wonderful, and it showed me that finishing what you start is a game changer. Do your best without apology and God will let your light shine. I don't remember my time for this ride (or if anyone kept track of the time) or if I passed any other bicyclists on the second day, but I certainly do remember this ride with unexpected gratitude and praise.

11

My Seven Year Dream

There came a time when Betty and Nick moved back to Mississippi, and life as a father began to make sense again. I made an earnest search for a better place to live so Nick would feel welcome and at home when he was with me.

My Uncle Jim bought a run-down house with two bedrooms and one bath and, in today's vernacular, flipped it into a better house. I bought this house and had Uncle Jim remove the floor furnace, which I considered too dangerous for a young child. He replaced it with a central air system which provided both air conditioning in the summer and heat in the winter, a much better solution. The house was on a dead-end street, also safer for Nick. My bathroom only had a 22" wide opening, not wide enough for my 23" wheelchair. It made no difference because the bathroom was too small for my chair to turn around in any way. I made do by leaving my chair outside the door and scooting around. I put in a 3-foot step stool so I could reach the sink and mirror. This was not an ideal setup, but one I could easily feel at home in and a solution I would use many times in the future. There was a washer/dryer hookup and I found a used set for the right price and had them installed. There was a carport for my vehicle. The house was everything I needed for comfort with homey space for my son.

The one thing I needed was a gas stove. Off I went to Sears. As I rolled into the store, I was met by a tall, attractive sales lady with a very pretty smile. She was confident and personable and helped me find the right stove for my house. We struck up a conversation and I invited her to dinner. She accepted.

Over dinner, I discovered that Paula Dianne and I were like-minded in Christ. I belonged to a Baptist Church and she belonged to an Assembly of God church a few miles down the road. We both belonged to choirs at our respective churches and were both filled with the Holy Spirit. Paula Dianne openly spoke in tongues, and I prayed in tongues quietly in my head. I never shared any of this with anyone at the Baptist church, because everyone knows the Baptists don't believe in speaking in tongues, at least not back in the mid-1990s. During the course of our dating, I switched to the Assembly of God, and immediately felt more comfortable and at home.

We had both made prior marital mistakes and were determined that we would date in a Godly way, which for us meant honoring each other by abstaining from sex. After dating for six months, I proposed to her. We were sitting in my pickup truck overlooking a beautiful, scenic lake and she lovingly accepted. We eloped shortly after that to Lake Village, Arkansas, where a Justice of the Peace married us.

I was happy with Paula Diane at the church we attended. We sang in the choir, and I got active in the Royal Rangers with my son. Royal Rangers is an activity-based, small group ministry for boys to teach them Godly ways of living and to equip and empower them to be Christlike men and servant leaders when they grew up. Our group included fathers, sons and grandfathers. Nick met the 5-year-old age requirement and I signed us up, thinking it would be a great way to bond within the framework of a church. It had the additional advantage of meeting on Sunday nights and I had visitation on most Sunday evenings. Nick and I would have many memorable Royal Ranger activities together.

We attended Ranger campout weekends whenever possible, doing all the campout activities that were part of such weekends, hiking (wherever I could hike in my chair that is), fishing and playing father-son games. There were outdoor church services aimed at enriching young boys' lives. We skipped bathing and went home stinky, dirty and happy every time.

One weekend there was a "Council-Fire" event. This is a special outdoor church service where everyone attends dressed in their Royal Ranger finest as Mountain Boys and Men of God. We arrived in our finest duds to see a large pile of logs and brush waiting to be lit. On command a fiery arrow was shot into the air and appeared to fly around the world. We watched the arrow fly away in one direction and then miraculously, it came around from the opposite direction to land in the logs and brush, where it instantly caught fire. It was spectacular and impossible to explain in a rational way. Our young Rangers loved it. It was at one of these outdoor events that I watched my son give his heart to Christ. I was overwhelmed with joy and gratitude that my young son had chosen Jesus for himself.

Paula Dianne and I were each busy with our own activities in church. As we got busier and more involved in church, we became less and less involved with each other. Her little habits began to grate on my nerves. She was late for everything, it didn't matter what. I am never late, I consider consistent tardiness to be self-centered rudeness, but Paula Dianne did not see it that way at all. If she was running a little late, I should cool my jets until she was ready to go. We could not discuss this lateness problem, because nothing changed. She would be late, I would get mad and pop off and we would drive in silence to our destination. The next time, it was the same thing. It irritated me to no end and never got better.

For distraction, I found myself wanting a motorcycle, but I wasn't sure what kind. I thought I might want to build my own, one that would accommodate my special physical needs. I started looking for a bike to modify. My father-in-law had an old Volkswagen Beetle floor pan out behind his barn. It was nothing more than a transmission, drive axle and engine. He gave it to me, and this became the starting point of what I would later call my Seven-Year-Dream. While I wrestled with how I was going to put this bike together, I stored it in the carport. I didn't have to worry about anyone stealing it, because it was nothing but pieces for a long time. I had a friend named Danny who owned a mobile welding service and we would talk about what needed to be done. But, in the beginning, it was mostly talk between us, and his encouragement for me to dig in and get started.

Paula Dianne was older than me and had two grown boys. Her youngest son was a Green Beret Marine sniper, and a personable young man. Her oldest son was married to an addict who would sneak into the house and steal jewelry and anything else that wasn't nailed down to support her habit. Even though we knew the thefts were taking place, Paula Diane would not confront or stop the thievery. This son and addict had a child named Amber who everyone spoiled and catered to, but no one disciplined. She was a demanding crying brat, and I could muster no sympathy at the time for the mother, the father or even the child. This codependent family was often at our home disrupting meals and my peace of mind.

Since there was never any peace in the home where I grew up, and since WG was still in the middle of my life, I found myself angry and resentful. I did not act like the man of God that I claimed to be and I certainly did not feel like it on the inside. I wanted to yell at the mother and spank the daughter and ended up nagging Paula Dianne to control her family that was driving me nuts. I stayed away from the house working on my trike as much as possible and avoided the conflict at home. And, then came that fatal-to-our-marriage Thanksgiving.

There were six of us there that holiday. Paula Dianne, her two sons, the addict wife, their daughter and me. The table was beautiful and loaded with a fabulous Thanksgiving feast that Paula Dianne had slaved over. There was an oven roasted turkey, potatoes, sweet potatoes, vegetables, and hot bread. Desserts were hidden in the kitchen, but I knew they were there, pumpkin pies and pecan pies. Whipped cream was in the fridge. My mouth was watering from the aromas and I was famished.

We said grace and sat down to eat when Amber started whining that she didn't want anything on the table. There was not one thing on the table that she would eat and demanded that her granny fix her mac and cheese. Grandma Paula Dianne got up from a table full of hot food and went to the kitchen to cook mac and cheese for Amber. I was furious and could not get past it.

In fact, I was so mad, I moved out and divorced Paula Dianne over it. I can look back now, years later, and see how ungodly I behaved. But at the time I couldn't handle this situation, the sick family interactions, including those between WG and me. Running away made a lot more sense, not that I would have admitted to it. I distracted myself by blaming WG and everyone else that was close to me, including Paula Dianne.

My Volkswagen trike became a healing distraction for me. When the chaos of yet another divorce was settled, and I was once again on my own, I would find that God was right there with me. He would show me the way and I would grow in the Lord and become a better man. I felt that I spent my entire adult life running to God and then running from God, and, in general, falling far short of what I thought I should be. So, I concentrated on building my trike.

Volkswagen trike conversions were popular in California. They tended to have long fiberglass, metal-flake painted bodies. They were cool and flashy, but that was not what I wanted. I wanted something different and practical. A trike that would look like something that Rod Kendrick would own, I just wasn't sure what that was. I wanted a trike for stability, but I wasn't a mechanic or an engineer.

> Be anxious for nothing, but in everything by prayer and supplication, with thanksgiving, let your requests be made known to God. Phil. 4:6 NKJV

I would pray at night before going to bed and ask God for direction on my project. Don't laugh. It worked. Every time I prayed for direction, I would dream of an answer. I didn't get a custom design for my entire bike all at one time, but I would get a solution for the problem I was currently working on. I don't know why I didn't ask for the same direction in my life.

Danny, my friend with the welding company, helped me piece by piece, one part at a time. We replaced the VW engine with a long-block engine that shipped from California. I found a scrapped motorcycle front end and frame from a 1980 Suzuki 750 GS. Danny was able to weld these items to my VW transaxle, securely and perfectly. My new seat was a NASCAR aluminum racing bucket seat. The motorcycle frame and the passenger seat blended into my design (or rather God's design). The foundation of my trike was now formed. Later I would add an expanded metal basket at the rear so I could carry my wheelchair.

All my work was done as I could afford it, paycheck to paycheck. Some components required money from several checks, but I didn't give up. I was determined to finish this trike and do it without using credit. Sometimes first efforts didn't work, and there were many adjustments. The wiring, braking system and controls came one small frustrating step at a time. I had to have total control of my trike using only my upper body strength and there were no specs for that.

My long-block engine was modified with high performance parts as my budget allowed. The wiring, braking system and controls were worked out as the project progressed. Again, I am not a mechanic, engineer, fabricator, builder or designer, but with God's help, the motorcycle began to take shape. God also brought me friends with special skills who would rekindle my love for this project and help me climb the next mountain of challenges.

Eventually, there came a day, years later, when I could see my bike, touch it, sit on it and start it. There were still challenges that confounded me. I kept my trike in a storage building for security. It gave me a place to work whatever the weather, and I liked spending time there, even when it was frustrating. One day I would start the engine and let it idle. Listening to the engine as I revved it always gave me a shot of adrenaline. I would check the oil pressure gauge, then the electrical charging system and confirm all was well. I would turn the ignition off, secure my tools and leave.

A week or so later I would return to work on my project and it would not start. Nothing had changed, just a few days had passed. This was so frustrating and happened over and over again. There were times I considered rolling my dream out of the storage unit and setting it on fire so I could be done with it. I didn't do that, of course, but I did find smarter people than me who could help fix what was wrong.

One afternoon while browsing the newspaper, I ran across an ad for the Christian Motorcycle Association (CMA). That immediately appealed to me as a ministry that I would enjoy and that God might be able to use me in. The first meeting I attended was at a small restaurant where we ate breakfast and then took a ride. My trike was still in the building stage, so I followed the bikers in my truck. Even though I was separated from the motorcycle column, I felt like part of the group. For several years I participated by following behind in my truck, then going home and working on my own motorcycle.

One of those friends I made in CMA was David. He was an electrical engineer and the perfect person to help with the wiring and detailed fabrication design of my trike. He saw my vision and improved upon it. He blessed me with his wisdom and encouragement. He helped me many times when the engine would not start, and he would tinker with this and that until the problem seemed to be solved. He would come back and help again when the bike would not start the next time. We became close friends. He never got discouraged and continued to encourage me when I threatened to roll the bike off a cliff.

Before my trike was fully roadworthy, I joined in a rally with CMA that took place in Natchez, MS. I drove my truck (that the bike world called a "cage") to the rally bringing up the rear of our highway formation. It may seem odd to travel in a vehicle to a rally, but once you are there, it makes no difference. Everyone parks their own vehicle and they walk everywhere (or push their wheelchairs, like me). There were a couple of hundred motorcycles, campers, a flatbed truck that served as a stage and bikers and families brought their own food and supplies. It was a memorable event for several reasons.

CMA set up their white-topped 24-hours/day canopy tent and served fresh coffee, water and Gatorade along with cookies, honey buns, gospel tracts and first-aid supplies. I was amazed at how God drew the lonely and the hurting into our tent. Men and women would stop by for a bottle of water or a cookie and stay to share their hurt and pain. We listened, we prayed. We comforted the hurting in the wild mayhem of a biker rally.

Motorcycle riders have families and they bring them to rallies. The kids ran wild, made immediate friends, and chased and played all day long. One of our lady bikers set up a face painting station under our tent and it drew the children like bees to flowers. Every child who came for a face painting was invited to our church service on Sunday morning.

Our CMA church service was conducted on the same stage that blared rock music the night before. There were bikers passed out here and there oblivious to the hustle and bustle of Sunday morning activities. The children were up laughing shrilly and running and playing. Grownups had their service at the stage and children were led to our CMA canopy tent for a devotional.

Because of my involvement with Royal Rangers, I had the delightful task of entertaining these wiggly, excitable kids who might or might not know Jesus Christ. I told them the story of the "Mother Hen and the Brush Fire". This is a touching story of a hen with chicks caught in a thunderstorm when a lightning bolt ignites a brush fire. The hen has no place to run and quickly gathers her chicks in her nest and covers them with her wings. The next day the landowner is walking through the damage caused by the fire when he finds the blackened nest and the dead hen. When he kicked the nest, all the baby chicks ran out chirping and looking for food.

As the children listened in amazed attention at how the chicks were saved from death by the love of their mother, I was able to ask them if they knew that Jesus had also died to save them. The Holy Spirit moved through my young group and after a while I invited them to pray the sinner's prayer of salvation. I was deeply touched by their earnest faces and their clasped hands. It was a joy to bring these little children into the Kingdom of God. I was blessed to have that opportunity to serve and that for all my mistakes, God would use me in such a humbling and tender way.

God used me in another way on the ride home. Again, I was at the back of the formation and there was a biker and his little daughter directly ahead of me. It was a warm day and the road was meandering and scenic. The little girl kept dozing off, her head tilting off to one side, and then she would jerk herself awake, only to nod off again a few minutes later. I became alarmed at the nods and jerks and was afraid that she might tragically fall off the bike and be killed. I honked and flashed my lights until I finally caught her dad's attention and he pulled over. After explaining what was happening and after Dad got a good look at his sleepy daughter, we transferred her to my truck and she slept safely and peacefully the rest of the way home. This was the first of many rallies that I attended with CMA.

Another memorable rally that I attended was "Blowout". This event was promoted by the "Asgard," a 1% motorcycle outlaw club. Their rally was held over the Memorial Day weekend and was an all-adult affair. It was most memorable not in a good way, but a wild ungodly way. There was security everywhere to provide safety. Wild music and alcohol revved the partygoers. Even with security, total chaos reigned. The rally was on the gulf coast at the Gulfport Dragway. There were 100 acres for camping and RVs were everywhere.

Even from outside of the park, it was obvious the weekend would be loud and lawless. I waited outside the gates in a line that barely crawled and ran the air conditioner on high. It was excruciatingly hot and humid, even for Mississippi. I was thankful that I hadn't come on my motorcycle. It was a furnace outside as the sun beat down from a clear blue sky and there was no breeze to offer relief. I watched excited rally goers drink beer outside the gates signaling that the party had started a quarter mile from the entrance.

All rally goers are given an armband to signify that their entry fee is paid. Inside the gate, it is pay as you go. There are charges for everything. Food, snacks, cold drinks, ice, beer, and firewood had been marked up to bring huge profits to the promoters. An outside shower was available for a price. It was in this atmosphere that CMA set up its white tent with all the usual free drinks, first aid, listening ears and open hearts for anyone that wanted prayer.

During the day, a bike show and wet t-shirt contest entertained those that chose to attend. I was shocked when over-eager female contestants removed their t-shirts to gain the crowd's approval. Nudity was rampant at the rally as beautiful, young women strutted throughout the campgrounds seeking approval from men who were only too ready to take advantage. There was much feigned shock from the laughing women who deftly moved out of the way of grabbing hands whenever possible.

A slender young girl wearing a white fur bikini approached the CMA tent. Alarm bells sounded in my head as she neared. Earlier another female rally goer had stripped off her shirt inside the CMA canopy and caused a flurry of action. I was prepared for another nude episode, but the young girl thankfully moved away. I was shocked at the exploitation of women at this rally. As a Christian man I needed to be fully prayed-up, and even though I had been warned, I still wasn't prepared for the reality.

I found myself thinking about the young girl in the fur bikini. I was embarrassed for her. I felt the pain of a father looking at his own young daughter. It was shocking to see her so exposed and vulnerable in a place of such depraved activity. God's compassion overwhelmed me and I prayed for her deliverance. The face of that young girl has stayed with me all these years and I have wondered what became of her.

Drag racing at night was a complete sensory explosion. The smoke from the burnouts combined with the pungent smell of burning rubber created fumes and exhaust that made the ¼ mile track impossible to see clearly. The noise from the crowd and the bikes was overwhelming. The lack of lighting in the staging lanes intensified the experience. Sweat rolled down my neck as I got swept into the excitement of the crowd jostling and bumping into me. By the time it was over, I was exhausted from the day and ready for sleep.

Camping in my tent brought no relief from the heat. I was forced to retreat to my truck and the comfort of the air-conditioning. The end of this rally could not come quickly enough! This was my first and last time to attend a 1% rally. Too much heat. Too much noise. Too much temptation and distraction.

I was glad to get back to work, to my quiet, controllable life and time to spend with God. My motorcycle was waiting for me and I was ready to have a go at it again.

When it seemed that I finally had a running bike, I applied to the State of Mississippi for a special VIN number for a homemade vehicle. With that VIN number I could ask for a Mississippi motor vehicle safety inspection. With that safety inspection, I could apply for a tag. With the tag, my Seven Year Dream (that had taken eleven years to build) was officially a road-worthy vehicle. This excited me beyond belief. This was official confirmation that I had accomplished what seemed like the impossible. I had taken a pile of discarded junk and with a little money, elbow grease and expertise from God and friends had built something tangible. All the frustrating hours of planning, working and turning wrenches became a distant memory. I was now a CMA biker on a mission and I was amazed at how God would use me.

I took my first road trip alone and went to Natchez, MS to a new restaurant on the bluffs overlooking the Mississippi River. It featured catfish and BBQ and was only 100 miles from home on the Natchez Trace Parkway. The traffic was light, especially for a Saturday, and no 18-wheelers were allowed on this two-lane road. The speed limit was 50 MPH and that gave me plenty of time to relax and enjoy the beautiful scenery and the performance of my trike.

Getting to the restaurant was simply a matter of following the road and the signs. It was such a relaxing ride that I was surprised to find that the parking lot was jam packed. To make matters worse, it was an unmarked gravel lot and cars were parked every which way in a haze of dust and grit. People were coming and going without looking. It was the definition of mayhem.

I had to park, dismount, and then load into my wheelchair. Between the bike and the front door was nothing but gravel and uneven grassy spots. My chair covered the distance in slow bumps and I looked out for hidden gravel holes. Before I lost my legs, none of this would have mattered one bit. Today

I set my mouth with grim determination and headed for the entrance. There was a thirty-minute wait to get in the door and seated and another thirty minutes before my order was delivered. Once seated I saw the spectacular scenery out of the large windows facing the west and I forgot about the mob, the dirt and the wait. The majestic muddy Mississippi rolled past while the sun shone in an azure sky. Golden sunbeams sparkled through white clouds over the river and through the trees. I enjoyed the view immensely and it made the trip one of those memorable events you remember all your life.

My catfish dinner was delicious, but nothing in comparison to the view. I paid my bill and left. There was no time to waste if I wanted to make it home before nightfall.

My shiny aluminum bucket seat caught the sunlight and I could see that my entire bike was covered in dust. As the engine roared to life, it was no longer purring with power. It was now sputtering and cutting out as I pulled out of the parking lot and onto the highway. As I accelerated, the engine died. I restarted my bike and again it died at 20 MPH. I restarted several more times but could not get my bike to run faster than 20 MPH before dying.

Finally, I pulled to the side of the road to figure out what to do. I felt panic. I was 100 miles from home and knew no one in this area. I was lucky enough to make it to a gas station where I got my bike off the road and could safely work on it. I discovered that the gas filter was completely clogged with sand and gravel, which meant somebody had opened my gas tank and put in a handful of dirt. I was so angry over this malicious destruction that I was speechless with rage. I was feeling so proud of my hard work and persistence and now this senseless thing had happened.

While I fumed over the damage to my motorcycle, a young man came up to me to offer help. He lived literally around the corner. I told him what was going on and he offered to let me park my machine at his home until I could return for repairs. I followed him home, my engine coughing and sputtering, and shut it down. I called my technical engineer buddy, David, and he came and got me. The next weekend we returned, flushed the gas tank and made a couple of other repairs. I was able to ride my bike home with David following me. I later installed a locking gas cap so this could never happen to me again. My Seven Year Dream was never dependable, always frustrating, and a learning experience that never quit teaching me to rely on God.

12

Make a Dollar, Spend Three

My life settled into a pleasant routine of time with my son, work and church. I was still active in CMA, and working on my motorcycle was a never-ending challenge. I continued to volunteer with Royal Rangers and have fun with Nick whenever possible. He was growing up fast and I didn't want to miss any of it.

My relationship with Jesus continued to grow and I got involved with a prison ministry. I got certified through the Department of Corrections to be a volunteer chaplain at the Central MS Correctional Facility in Pearl where men and women served one year or less prison sentences. I also served at the notorious Parchman Correctional Facility in the Mississippi River Delta area. At Parchman I only served the men on death row, and it was an experience totally different than I expected.

The atmosphere on death row was dark and the entire building smelled oddly. I could never determine what that smell was, but it was always disconcerting. There was very little lighting and no windows. Bars were everywhere and there were multiple barred doors to go through. Once inside it was dismal and there was a depressing sense of doom. There was no public meeting area so we met outside of each cell. There were a few Christian inmates and we prayed together. I was surprised that they wanted to pray over me as much as I wanted to pray over them.

Death row is where I encountered my first Muslim prisoner. We talked but we could never reach an understanding. To him Jesus would never be more than another prophet, but our exchanges were respectful and more philosophical than I expected.

Every time I left, I felt that I was being blessed more than I was blessing. That was something I never expected and the reward for serving in this area was intense in my life. On one of the van rides home from visiting Parchman, every person aboard felt the same way that I did. We were blessed more by the inmates than we could ever bless them. We rode home in the sweet afterglow of serving God. This was only one of many times, and this aspect never changed.

This is where I would like to tell you that I had surrendered my total life, body and soul to Jesus Christ, that I never made any more stupid mistakes and that the rest of my journey has been a righteous story of serving Christ. I would be lying.

I was working for the same company that had hired me after I left the Mississippi State Park System. It was a different branch, but the same company. I was still part of Christian Motorcycle Association. I was still involved in my Assembly of God church. I was restless in my "busy-ness". I was constantly searching for fulfillment, but nothing satisfied my soul. My prison ministry only filled a portion of the fulfillment I was looking for. Even with God opening amazing doors for me, I was not at peace. I didn't know it then, but I was about to open the door and invite insanity in.

I was sitting in a Sunday School class for adults one day when a beautiful, blue-eyed, platinum blonde walked into the room. Every face in the class turned toward her and stayed there. She was wearing form fitting jeans and a shirt with a hint of cleavage showing. It was the slight shimmer of sparkle on her face, her self-assured carriage that screamed "look at me," that held every man's eyes. I was immediately guilty of lusting after her along with every other man in the room.

She smiled at me and sat nearby. Her attention was flattering. Her flirting was unexpectedly disarming because she directed it at me when there were plenty of other single men in the room. I found myself captivated by her warm Southern charm and her infectious laughter. She wasn't put off by my wheelchair and I began to look forward to those Sunday School lessons for reasons that had nothing to do with God's Word. I was headed down the road of destruction, and when I looked at her, I was totally blinded.

Within a month I asked Rebekah out, and she happily accepted. She was fun, there was no getting around that. With her infectious laughter and gentle touches to my arms and face, all my reserve melted away. Our dates were always time constricted as Rebekah's mother was an invalid and Rebekah was her chief caregiver. Our dates were dinners together or talking over coffee. Sometimes, we took in a movie. I took her to meet my mother and WG, who was also charmed by Rebekah's sweet attention. At the end of that visit, my mother simply whispered in my ear, "Red Flags, Rod, Red Flags." I heard what she said, but totally dismissed it as irrelevant.

I should have listened to my mother. What she saw immediately, I never saw until it was too late. Rebekah was spoiled and nagged relentlessly to get what she wanted. She was laser focused in her pursuit of pricey things. Every 'want' became a 'need' that had to be filled.

Life was rosy as long as she got her way. I didn't see any of this, and even if I had, I wouldn't have cared. I focused on satisfying her every whim.

Rebekah was a PK (Preacher's Kid). She was the youngest child of a two-child family. Her daddy gave her everything she wanted and spoiled her rotten. She once informed me that it was my job to give her everything she wanted, just like her daddy had done. I probably laughed when she said it without realizing that she was dead serious. What I didn't give, she would later take. I was so smitten that I could see none of this. If there were alarms and bells that went off, I didn't hear them. I didn't want to get married again, but when she pushed for marriage, I didn't break it off. I postponed the discussion, but only temporarily. I had become a 'want' that she 'needed,' and nothing but marriage would suffice.

Eventually, I relented and we married. From the beginning our marriage had lots of unresolved issues, mostly dealing with money. There was nothing financially out of her reach and her reach extended to the bottom of my pockets until there was nothing left but lint. No amount of protest on my part kept her from spending.

There were some wonderful things about Rebekah. She was a loving and tender caregiver to her mother. She was patient and willing while she ministered to her every need, especially as her life began to slip away. After our marriage, I moved in with her so that Rebekah could give her mother the total care that she needed. Every day she would get her mother up, bathe her, fix her hair, dress her and prepare all her meals. She would chat with her, pamper her and watch hours of golf on television with her because her mother loved it. At the end of the day, she would tuck her into bed and the next day, she would do it all over again. When her mother died, Rebekah truly grieved her passing. I did not and will never fault my bride for this loving attention to her mother.

Her mother's estate went through probate with the usual estate sales, etc. Rebekah's share of the estate was approximately $15,000. She blew through that money within three months. We ate out every night. There were wild spending sprees. The money was totally hers to do with as she wanted and I had no right to tell her what to do with it. I was amazed at how quickly she spent every dime. My mother's admonition in my ear, "Red Flags, Rod, Red Flags" began to hit home.

Shortly after that, I was offered a transfer to a branch in Tulsa, Oklahoma. This would mean a lot more money and a chance to move to a more urban area. It would also mean a chance to put more distance between WG and me. We were flown into Tulsa and given the royal treatment by my company. Rebekah shamelessly flirted and charmed my General Manager. She loved being treated like the queen and reveled in the fancy restaurants and our hotel accommodations. Rebekah and I discussed this promotion and move and decided that the time was right to try something new. I happily accepted the job offer. The move was on and we looked forward to this new adventure.

We packed, said goodbye to Mississippi and headed to Oklahoma. We moved into an apartment and began to settle into a place where WG would no longer be able to drop in unannounced and create havoc. That single thought gave me an inordinate amount of peace. For the first time in my life, I was truly out from under WG's thumb. I had a beautiful wife who supported the move (and the money, of course) and a job I was excited to start. I found myself loving Tulsa and that has never changed, even though there have been a great many changes since moving here.

My Seven-Year Dream moved with us and I tucked her away in a storage unit close to the apartment. My motorcycle was still unreliable and a pain in my neck, but the truth is that so much time, money and love had gone into making her run that I had to keep her. Time on the motorcycle was my "face in the wind time" exploring the beautiful areas around Eastern Oklahoma. There was peace and solace on the back of that bike and the wonderful smells of Oklahoma were refreshing. I was a guy on a bike. I loved the low humidity of the area. Rebekah never rode with me even though she claimed to love bikers and even though there was a seat for her. The bike was my peace. My solitude. My time with God Almighty.

I searched for a local chapter of the Christian Motorcycle Association, but, sadly, could not connect. My solitary rides continued. I still had the problem of "Will the bike start today?" Maybe "Yes." Maybe "No." I did spend a lot of time at the storage unit tinkering and puttering around. It was peaceful. When the weather was warm, I loved it there.

Our apartment was located conveniently close to work. The General Manager at work was a great guy I was happy to work for. I liked the company and enjoyed the increase in pay, even though the cost of living was slightly higher in Oklahoma. Rebekah was a great cook and there was a hot meal waiting for me every night when I got home. Eventually, we found a home church where Rebekah was comfortable (meaning there weren't too many good-looking women, so she would still be a standout). I thought we might be happy here, but once again I was wrong.

Without going into a lot of ugly details, I could not provide my wife with the style of living that she was used to. She had been spoiled as a child and grew up thinking she was entitled to have everything she wanted. Even if I had wanted to, I could never have attained the standard of living that she wanted. Things began to disappear from around the house. Nothing big, at first. Eventually, she pawned everything of value, including her own wedding ring to support her fantasy lifestyle. If there was $100 in the bank, she would spend $300. I borrowed money against my next paycheck to cover the overdrafts, but I could not keep up with the wild spending. There were times when I "borrowed" a roll of toilet paper from work because we were out and there wasn't any money until payday. It was humiliating, infuriating and love killing. In my mind Rebekkah went from this sparkling, beautiful woman with a big heart for her mother to a whining, manipulating nag obsessed with spending whatever it took to keep her looking as beautiful as possible.

She became jealous of every woman I talked to. A mere nod of the head to a woman at church meant hours of screaming at home. She accused me of unfaithfulness, which was false. Every time I brought up the subject of reduced spending, she countered with my untrustworthiness. It took me a while to see that this was her way of deflecting the subject away from money. This unhappiness went on for months with both of us stumbling forward, me working to cover costs and her spending more than I could ever hope to make.

We did try to work things out. I wasn't a complete scrooge with money even though I had always lived within my means. One afternoon I took Rebekah to a PBR (Pro Bull Riding) qualifying rodeo in Tulsa. It was a chance to get out and maybe have a good time. We both looked forward to it so the evening started out smoothly. We got our seats and enjoyed the first riders. My wife was happily smiling when I excused myself to go get her a drink. The lines were long and took forever. I made it worse by deciding to buy her a souvenir shirt. I knew she would like it and wear it to remember the evening. That line also took forever.

By the time I got back to my wife, her relaxed and smiling face had turned savage and dark. She stood up and accused me of flirting with every woman and stormed out of the arena. She stomped out to the parking lot with me chasing her, and she hopped in the truck and roared out of the parking garage.

I sat there in shocked exasperation. She had left me fifteen miles away from home at ten o'clock at night in a wheelchair. I was furious. I pushed my chair at least two full miles before I found a phone I could use. I will spare you the humiliating details of getting home that night, but when I opened my front door, the last thing I expected to see was the barrel of a gun pointed straight at me and my wife's face contorted in rage.

I slammed the door shut and never went back. Rebekah returned to Mississippi. We divorced. I swore I would never marry again. I was mad and hurt and disappointed. I was broke beyond broke and my credit was destroyed for years. I was again a failure in every sense of the word. The only thing I had left was God and I hung on to him for dear life. It took years to restore my meager credit rating. It took longer than that for me to heal emotionally. Men don't talk about their feelings, it is too humiliating. I don't like admitting that I was as co-dependent as any woman with an alcoholic husband, just in a different way. If you are a man who is caught in this kind of trap, when I say, "I feel your pain," I mean "I really feel your pain! You are not alone."

I took comfort in the Word of God. This was the only thing that gave me any hope.

Paul wrote in Romans 8:18:

> "For I consider that the sufferings of this present time are not worthy to be compared with the glory which shall be revealed in us."

Paul spoke directly to me. I needed to know this for my everyday struggles and peace of mind. Slowly, my pain subsided. My anger and humiliation became bearable. My shame was a hidden agony and my only peace came in God's Word. I kept at it until it began to sink in, until I could feel it in my bones. It took time, way longer than I thought it should. It also took time for me to forgive myself for being so blindly stupid about another woman.

13

The Quiet After The Storm

After Rebekah left, I withdrew to find myself again. I moved to a smaller, more money wise one-bedroom apartment. It was wheelchair accessible and I moved in. Most of my meals were simple fare, oatmeal for breakfast, a sandwich for lunch, and for dinner something I cooked in the crock pot for dinner. I spent a lot of my free time in God's Word and an equal amount of time parked quietly in front of the TV. During the week I got up and went to work and then came home. On weekends I went to church. Slowly, I paid off the mountain of debt and got financially stable. I did not date or even look at women.

For me it was a matter of "Do the next right thing." I had an old friend named Doug back in Mississippi. We would talk for hours about how to figure out what the next right thing was. We tried to figure out if we should get advice from a lot of people, only a few people or no one. I finally decided the only one I could count on for good advice was God, as I surely had given myself bad advice over the years. I spent more time in God's Word learning how to incorporate his Word into my life.

I longed for a new motorcycle. For a long time, I couldn't afford to consider the possibility. But finally, there came a day when it was possible. I wanted one that was dependable and would start every time. I decided to get rid of my 7-year dream. It was so aggravating, starting sometimes, not starting most of the time. I couldn't sell it even though I tried. There was a former Formula One driver who had a storage unit down a couple of units from me. We would chat from time to time and I found out he had a small farm. He was looking for some kind of vehicle that he could use to get around on his acreage. I gave him my unreliable motorcycle with full disclosure about its unreliable nature. In spite of that, he seemed delighted to get it and I was just as delighted to get rid of it.

Now the search was on for just the right motorcycle. I wanted a Harley-Davidson, that was the only thing I had firmly decided. I browsed on-line and at both of the Harley shops in Tulsa. I wanted the biggest and "baddest" bike possible, but those were way out of my price range. I finally found a 1200 cc Harley Sportster at a year-end close out sale that would fill the bill, and I bought it. It was delivered to my apartment and it sat there in my living room for several weeks. I firmed up my plans for modifying it to meet my physical limitations.

I needed to modify the gear shift and the braking system so that I could control my Sportster with my hands. I found a suicide jockey shifter online and was able to install it myself. This was the same kind of device I had installed on my 7-year dream so this was not a new experience for me. The braking system was another detail that did require expertise to properly install. A local Harley mechanic connected the front and the rear braking system into a new larger master cylinder with a proportioning valve to control both wheels. This allowed the front and the back wheel brakes to engage simultaneously and stop the bike safely.

The next thing that needed to be done was to add a platform for my wheelchair. This would be similar to a sidecar in that it would mount directly to my bike on one side and have a wheel on the outside. I wanted a platform with a ramp so I could roll onto it and transfer to the bike. This required special fabrication and it took a bit of time to find a company that would take on the job. I finally found one just outside of Paris, Texas. I borrowed a trailer from work and a friend helped me roll my bike from the apartment onto the trailer. I tied it down and headed south, I left Tulsa as excited as any kid with a new toy. With the platform installed, I would be able to safely mount my bike and ride again.

The plan was to drive to Texas, have my platform installed and return to Oklahoma the next afternoon. My part was easy, but the fabricator had a much tougher time. He had never done a project like mine, so the installation was more complicated than he had imagined it would be. He installed sidecars all the time, but a platform instead of a sidecar was different. Eventually, it was installed with minor adjustments and I was called to give it a test drive.

The minute my motorcycle roared to life, I got a jolt of adrenaline. As I pulled carefully out of the lot, the wind hit my face.

Joy and freedom coursed through my blood. I was unhindered. I could feel the power of my bike beneath me. With my wheelchair strapped beside me, I had complete and utter freedom to go anywhere, anytime, anyplace. A whole new and free world opened before me.

I enjoyed the afternoon ride so much that I kept riding. It was more than just a test drive, it was a freedom ride for my soul. Eventually, I forced myself to head back to the fabricator. I knew I still had a four-hour drive to Tulsa. My fabricator helped me load the bike on my trailer and I headed north with a joyful heart.

Once back in Tulsa, I was able to unload my motorcycle into my secured storage unit by myself. It was a wondrous experience to be able to do what I wanted and needed to do without always having to rely on someone else's help. As I headed home that night, I thanked God for providing the way and the means to control my own movements.

I began to look for a motorcycle ministry to join. The church I was currently attending didn't have one. I knew that God would use me to witness, and that my modified bike would draw people. After searching around the area, I found God's Shining Light. It had a large motorcycle ministry called The Priesthood. I didn't know anything about this ministry, but I was curious enough to go find out.

The first time I attended, I drove my truck into the parking lot and was amazed at the number of Harley-Davidson motorcycles parked around the building. The bikers themselves looked like bikers everywhere, black leathers, tattoos, heavy jewelry and bandanas. What I wasn't prepared for were the open, smiling faces or the gauntlet of shaking hands that reached from outside all the way into the church and the sanctuary. I was amazed. Nowhere had I ever been treated so warmly. I found a home the very first time I attended.

My new pastor, Dixie Pebworth, was a Biblical preacher. The final authority was Jesus Christ and his Word–whether you liked it or not. He was just my kind of preacher. God's Shining Light had a vast array of ministries that served its members and The Priesthood supported and raised money for all of them. This was something that would give some purpose to my life.

In the beginning I got involved with Celebrate Recovery as I was still trying to get out from under WG's thumb even though there was 600 miles between us. I was also still recovering from my latest marriage failure. Even though during this time my relationship with Jesus Christ was strong, I was far from healed, but ready for God to deal with me in his own way. I joined Celebrate Recovery and got a totally different slant than from any other 12-Step program. Here Jesus Christ was the openly proclaimed "Higher Power."

Meetings were congenial. There was a casual dinner at a great price before every meeting. As a single, non-cooking man that dinner was a big draw. There was a large group meeting followed by break-out small groups the second hour. Every other week there was a speaker who would give his testimony. I liked the set up, the people and the idea of healing with direction.

I met Vienna at a Celebrate Recovery meeting after she gave her testimony. She had grown up in a dysfunctional family and carried her dysfunction into several disastrous marriages. She was open and straightforward about the terrible choices she had made in her life. She was taking her healing day by day with God's help. She had been coming to GSL for a year or so, but I didn't remember ever seeing her until that night.

I ran into Vienna at CR almost every week. We'd visit and move on. She was very curious about my Harley and how it worked. I finally showed her how the ramp swung down and I rolled up onto the platform so I could lock my chair down and flip the ramp up. She was impressed with how my design had come together into a working piece of equipment. I was impressed that she asked so many questions and seemed genuinely interested.

Sometimes we ate together. It wasn't planned. It just happened. We'd talk. We got to know each other and gradually became friends. She was hard working and had a good education. She was sharp and I was impressed that she knew a lot of things most women didn't know. There were similarities in our jobs, so we talked about inventory and freight problems and how to solve them. There were times when we commiserated over the bad choices we had made. Vienna was a no-nonsense woman who could laugh at herself as easily as she could stand up for herself. We were both committed to a deeper relationship with God and finding a healthier way to live.

Over time I noticed that Vienna was different from the other women I had known. We had a lot in common, not silly stuff like we both liked the same music or apple pie. She was honest to the core. In the year that I had known her, I never once caught any discrepancy. She had learned to live within her income and make do. She was a "full tither" and God would take care of her needs if she did her part. She was politically a right-wing conservative, just like me. She had a lot of opinions on a lot of topics and I was surprised that our opinions ran parallel most of the time.

Then, a friend t0 both of us in our church was shot in his front yard while taking out his trash. Jack was a big man and tough looking. Why some scrawny guy would decide to rob someone big enough to squash him like a bug is hard to imagine. He demanded Jack's wallet and when Jack laughed at him, he shot Jack, twice. His life was hanging by a thread. Our church prayed for him until he made it over the hump, but he had months of healing ahead of him before he could go back to work.

The Priesthood threw a fundraiser for him and I invited Vienna to go with me. That is when I finally asked for her phone number. As we made plans, she admitted that she had never been on a motorcycle and was leery of going now. I offered to do the scripture run in the truck, but she relented and we made plans to take the motorcycle. We met at the church on the appointed Saturday and I was surprised that she came with all the necessary gear. My Priesthood sisters had come up with a helmet, full leathers and gloves. The weather was chilly and she came layered up and her hair tied in a bandana. I was impressed.

There was no backseat on my Harley, so I seat belted her into my wheelchair and away we went with our group of twenty bikes. She laughed and waved all day long at other bikers and at cars that waved to her. She made the run at each stop for our scriptures so I never had to get off the bike. At the end of the run we ate spicy chili, drank hot coffee and listened to Christian music. As the sun was going down I helped her load her borrowed gear into the back of her car and waved as she drove off. I knew I would ask her out again.

Over the months we grew closer and closer. We fell in love. She would hint around about our relationship and ask, "Where are we going with this?" I always responded with, "No pressure. Let's have fun." No matter how much I cared about her, there was no way I was ever going to get married again. I couldn't bring myself to say that to her because I didn't want to risk losing her. I didn't want to hurt her but I was never going to put my head in another marriage noose again.

In the spring of 2015, I purchased a black GTI with cool mags that caught the attention of everyone I knew. I loved its sleek style and the immediate response of the engine. It had paddle shifters and I learned to shift like a race car driver. The thrill of driving that GTI is one of my fondest memories during that time.

Vienna loved that car, too, and we often went for drives in the car instead of on the Harley. She told me with mock flattery, "You look great behind the wheel of this car." We would chat and visit and enjoy the smooth ride and easy power of my car.

We'd stop for coffee and pie or for ice cream. At the end of the evening, I would take her home. As I watched her stroll to her door, I would make plans for the next date.

14

Healing and Grace

Vienna and I went to church together, Celebrate Recovery together and eventually, she moved into the same apartment complex that I lived in. Her apartment was far removed from mine, but still just up the hill. We did all the usual dating things, picnics and motorcycle rides. I even installed a proper seat for her to safely ride on. We had casual dates at the apartment pool. There were lots of dinners and cozy chats over coffee. We hit the museums together and Driller ball games in the springtime before it got Oklahoma hot in the summer.

Our relationship became so comfortable that I found myself withdrawing from it. I felt pressured even when she wasn't saying anything. I was curt at times, but she seemed to roll with it. Sometimes I hurt her feelings and she'd wince, but always got over it quickly. I didn't want to hurt her, but I was trying to protect myself. It was a fine line I was walking. I wanted her close, just not too close. One day I was especially short with her and she cried a couple of times. With my usual guy thinking, I figured the less I said about it, the better. She wasn't one of those "cry to get your way women," and she hardly ever cried, except at sappy TV ads and tear-jerker movies.

When I took her home that evening, her face was miserable. She looked at me with tears rolling down her cheeks and said, "You have broken my heart with the ugly things you said to me today. Your hatefulness is unacceptable." I was immediately ashamed of myself and apologized profusely. She had always been quick to forgive and forget so I moved on and casually said, "I'll pick you up at ten in the morning for church."

She shocked me when she said, "I don't think so." She quietly opened the door, tears streaming down her face and walked to her apartment without looking back.

Those four words hurt worse than I ever expected and I blew my top. I slammed the GTI into reverse and hit the gas. I screeched to a halt and slammed into first gear and screamed the car all the way down the hill to my place. I could not believe that she had dumped me. I didn't want her too close, but I never thought she would throw me under the bus. I did not want to get married. I wanted to have my cake and eat it, too. How dare she! I immediately built a wall between us as thick as I could make it.

She knocked on my door a week later and wanted to talk to me. I shut the door in her face. When I finally did talk to her a few weeks later, I said the meanest things I could think of, "Loving you is a lot of work and not much fun." I continued, "You've put on some weight." I knew that her weight had been a big issue in the past. I knew full well that she had been loved for how she looked and not who she was. Her response?

"I can't reconcile the sweet man I have been dating with the hateful things you have said to me lately. What happened to you? Where is my Rod," she looked at me earnestly. I shrugged my shoulders and kept my mouth shut. After a short time she turned and walked away. I felt like a heel, but I was not about to open any doors again.

We didn't talk after that. I had been trying to avoid getting into a tangled emotional mess that would lead where I had no intention of ever going again. At the same time, I wanted to hurt her like she hurt me. I would catch her looking at me in church with the saddest face, but I stayed away from her. I hardly spoke to her for the next year and a half. A season of loss was upon me and I thought I was tough and prepared for anything. I was not.

A short four months later, my beautiful GTI was T-boned going through an intersection. A driver ran a red light and plowed into me. My beautiful car was totally destroyed. I wasn't hurt, but it took several minutes for my senses to return. I popped the hatch and slowly worked my way back to to. I set my wheelchair out in the middle of the scene of the accident. Then I climbed out the back of the car and into my chair.

I looked at my car in despair. There were pieces of it strewn all over the intersection. I saw faces with open mouths staring at me with shocked expressions. I must have been dazed for a while because the police were already at the scene and came running toward me to help. Suddenly, EMT's were checking me out and there were dozens of questions about how I felt, where did I hurt, did I always get in and out of my vehicle through the rear hatch. First responders insisted that I take the ambulance to the hospital and get checked out from head to toe. As I sat woefully in the back of the ambulance, I said good-by to the nicest car I had ever owned.

The hospital confirmed that I was intact and unhurt. When they released me the job of finding new transportation became an urgent necessity. I settled on a saffron Nissan Rogue, used, but with low mileage and as clean as a whistle. In some ways it was nicer than the GTI. It had a smoother ride, more room, backup cameras and a navigation system. Even as I settled into driving the Rogue, I missed the thrill of my sporty GTI.

In the Spring of 2016, my mother died. We had always been close and talked often. I loved her with every bone in my body. She had always been there for me, always supportive and encouraging. Over the years, I spent as much time with her as I could. Even WG couldn't keep me away. Thankfully, she had finally divorced him and was living free of the physical abuse she had suffered for decades. She was living in Germantown with her three long-haired dachshunds. I was stunned by her sudden and unexpected death.

My sister Shawn was supposed to get together with Mom for a weekend. When Shawn couldn't get in touch with her before that weekend, she came to Germantown anyway. Mom was lying on the couch peacefully dead. Calls went out to my sister

Renee and to me. I didn't pack much and was on the road within the hour.

The next week was a painful blur of activities. Mom was cremated. It was hard to make plans for a regular funeral service because we all lived in different states. We finally decided that at another time the three of us would fly out to California and scatter her ashes over the ocean. In the meantime, Renee would take the ashes to Florida for safekeeping. We stayed at Mom's house while we went through her things. We visited and drank endless cups of coffee while my mom's small treasures were doled out. WG was not invited and did not make an appearance.

It was a miserable experience. I came home with a car full of family paintings that my mother's mother had painted. I only met that grandmother one time in my entire life, and I had no recollection of her. There were also a couple of small kitchen appliances and one unique coffee mug. That was all I had to show for a lifetime of love and support.

Entering my empty apartment with one less person who I loved brought me no comfort. I was lonely and there was no relief.

A few months later I began to have problems with my right arm. It hurt and tingled and I had less and less movement. I relied on that arm heavily for loading and unloading my wheelchair into and out of the Rogue. I had a hard time pushing my chair at work and everywhere else I needed to go. In the shower I had limited movement and couldn't grip the towel to dry off. I could not lift my arm above my waist. It was time to find out what was wrong.

I scheduled an appointment with Tulsa Bone & Joint. They scheduled an immediate MRI that showed my spine looked like a crooked snake. Vertebrae 4, 5 and 6 in my neck had broken completely down. This caused my grip strength to be only 25% of normal. Surgery to correct my problem was scheduled as soon as possible. Until then, I had to roll my chair with one hand. I was miserable, in fact, everything about my life at this time was miserable.

My surgeon fused my damaged vertebrae together and then inserted a protective cage around them to stabilize movement and return function. I did have to do some rehab, but function was immediately restored and as my panic settled down, my gratitude returned for what God was doing for me. After a few weeks, I seemed as good as new.

The following August Vienna softly knocked on my door. When I opened the door she said, "I have bad news for you and I want you to hear it from me, not see it on Facebook." I was puzzled at her seriousness. I had hardly spoken to her in the last year. "Can I come in for a few minutes?" I let her in and she sat quietly next to me on the couch and said, "Thumper has died from a heart attack."

I sat in stunned silence as the news sank in. Thumper was my Priesthood sponsor. He was my CR sponsor. He was my friend and one of the few people who I trusted enough to confide in. As tears streamed down my face, she wrapped her arms around me and said nothing. Thumper was the only one who knew I still loved Vienna and would listen when I complained every time I saw her talk to another man, or if I even thought she was going out with someone else. He often got sick of my complaining and told me to "Man up, quit griping about it and shut up," as only a best friend can.

Vienna patted my back while I tried to come to grips with yet another loss. When I quieted down, she rose from the sofa, "I am so very sorry for your loss, Rod. I know you were close." She left as quietly as she had come. I saw her at the funeral, but we didn't speak.

The last few months were a nightmare of losses for me and I knew I needed God to help me get myself together. I could see that Vienna still loved me by her act of kindness about losing Thumper, but I had not changed my mind about marriage. No way did I want another failed marriage and the only way to avoid that was to never marry again. I began to pray for her, earnestly, that God would show her clearly what her destiny was so that she could move on. I didn't bother to pray that God would show me what my destiny was. Guys don't think like that.

I would see Vienna in church. She might look at me and smile, but then she would turn away. I could see she was sad, and of course, I presumed she was sad over me. I am a typical guy. I prayed harder for her.

A few weeks later I felt led to send her some flowers for her kindness to me. I sent her a dozen beautiful long-stemmed red roses from the most expensive and exclusive shop in town. She called immediately, "Rod, what are you doing? I just got roses from you. What for?" she demanded.

"Well, I don't know. I just thought it would be nice," I lamely responded. She hung up. When I rolled up to my apartment door that afternoon, the roses were sitting on my porch with a note that said, "leave me alone." I was shocked! I had expected her to fall all over herself at the chance to make up with me. Even if we never dated again, we could be friends.

The very next week, I sent her another dozen roses, this time white. Again, she called and again I had no decent response. She hung up on me. I really don't know what I was thinking. Two dozen roses had cost a fortune and I didn't have a fortune to waste. Where Vienna was concerned, I was in a fog. Loved her. Didn't love her. I didn't want to get married again. What did I want? I didn't know. I prayed harder for her. Again and again, I prayed that God would direct her path in another direction and away from me. "Dear God, show Vienna her destiny." I felt pretty good about that prayer. I don't know why I kept praying. It was now twice as obvious that she wasn't looking to get back together.

Late summer moved into fall. My life continued in work and church, study and prayer. I began to feel more hopeful about my future and the plans God had for me. I sought God's face in the midst of my recent losses. I trusted that God would open doors and shut others and that my life would begin to make sense again.

One morning after Sunday service several weeks later, Vienna walked up to me and with a smile on her face blurted out, "You are my destiny." For just a second, she had this happy look on her face, and in the next instant it was replaced with a look of horror, "Oh, Lord…" she started, then turned and ran for the exit.

I sat in stunned silence, and then, like a thunderclap my brain fog cleared and I rolled after her like a marathoner in my prime. I roared her name as I pushed my chair. I will never forget the guarded look on her face as I rolled near to her.

"We have to talk," I said and she responded, "About what? I never meant to say that to you." I could see that she was red-faced in her embarrassment and on the verge of tears.

My heart melted, "I have been praying for you for months that God would show you your destiny. Out of your own mouth, God is showing me that you are my destiny and I am yours." I could see that she wasn't buying it, but also that she was listening. That was all I needed. God turned my heart around in an instant, totally. I was no longer afraid of commitment or failure.

It didn't happen overnight, but rather over months. I proposed to her one night during Christmas time at Guthrie Green in downtown Tulsa. We had eaten dinner at a favorite Mediterranean place and then decided to walk through the park. There were dozens of other couples out enjoying the night. It was a beautiful, unusually warm December evening and the park was lit with thousands of twinkling lights. I got down on my only knee to ask her. She said, "Yes."

Vienna and I married six months later and God has shown me a thousand ways we are compatible. God is the third leg of our three-legged stool and gives us sweet peace and joy at home. Because we are solidly together with God in charge, he has called us both into more active service.

God had shown me that no matter how many times I have failed in the past, that when I put my trust in Him, He has my best welfare in his heart. He has shown me that He is not through with me yet, there are other hurting souls that He wants to touch and He is using us individually and together to reach out in His healing name.

Vienna and I have been married for almost six years. For the first time in my life, I know that I am married for the last time. I know that for every lousy mistake I have made in the past, God has used that mistake to help me comfort and encourage someone else. Our marriage is strong and because of that, we are each free to serve God in new and different ways.

One of my favorite things to do is ride. I admit I am much more of a fair-weather rider than some of my CMA friends. I have a trike now. It is much more comfortable and I feel safer on it. I have had it modified a couple of times, and because I am a true Harley-Davidson biker, there is always another modification around the corner. When I ride with CMA, what I love is that when we stop as a group, there is always someone who will approach me, drawn by the wheelchair on the back of my trike. Everybody knows someone who has gone through a loss and my chair and the loss of legs draws them to me. They have questions and they ask them. Every ride is a chance to witness for Jesus, to praise Him for His awesome healing powers and to encourage others going through their own troubles.

I never miss a chance to visit with a person who has lost a limb and is recovering in the hospital. It doesn't matter how the limb was lost. It could be from diabetes or a bike wreck. I remember how I felt, so angry and lost. Everyone who tried to encourage me had an intact body, so how could they know how it felt. God has used me to encourage someone grieving a lost limb just by showing up on my Harley. Words aren't always necessary as I pull my chair off the back of my bike and easily transfer from bike to chair. I can see the change and the hope on that face as I wheel toward him. My prayer is that God will expand this ministry all over the country. God helped me in spite of myself, my stupid decisions, my quick temper, my failed marriages and my miniscule amount of faith.

> "I say unto you, if ye have faith as a grain of mustard seed, you shall say unto this mountain, Remove hence to yonder place, and it shall remove; and nothing shall be impossible unto you." Matt 17:20 KJV

15

My Memorial Stone Altar

My altar is not a real rock altar, but rather reminders that God has moved in my life and answered prayers. They are memories that have evolved over the years from a note, a slip of paper, even concert ticket stubs. They are made up of answered prayers from the divine and powerful promises that God has given me. They are also documentation that God has used a pastor, another person or a simple event to touch my heart and change my life. My memorial stones are the basis of this book.

I need to remember every time that God has done something special for me so that <u>I never forget</u>. With these memorial stones, my faith will always have hard evidence of what God has done for me in the past. I thought I would share this with you in the hopes that it will encourage you to write down the special times in your life that Jesus has intervened on your behalf so that <u>you never forget</u>.

> Joshua 4:7 ends with: "...so these stones shall become a memorial to the children of Israel forever." (NKJV)

Stone One – JESUS

Everything in my life that makes sense starts with Jesus. If I could have only one stone, it would be Jesus. Jesus is my everything. He is my sure foundation. He is my lamp and lights the way. He is my savior, redeemer, messiah, healer, and friend. Without him I am totally lost and in the dark. He is my alpha and omega, the beginning, and the end. He is my rock.

> "Behold, I lay a stone for a foundation, a tried stone, a precious cornerstone, a sure foundation, whoever believes will not act hastily." Isa 28:16 NKJV

> "Therefore, it is also contained in the Scripture,
>
>> "Behold, I lay in Zion
>> A chief cornerstone, elect, precious,
>> And he who believes in Him will by no means be put to shame.
>
> "Therefore, to you who believe, He is precious; but to those who are disobedient,

> "The stone which the builders rejected
> Has become the chief cornerstone,
> And
>
> "A stone of stumbling
> And a rock of offense."
> "They stumble, being disobedient to the word, to which they also were appointed." 1 Pet. 2:6-8 (NKJV)

Jesus was the stone that was rejected by others, but He became the chief cornerstone for me. Falling in love with Jesus changed everything. When this happened for me, my willingness to serve exploded within my heart. As an example, while attending a Baptist Church in Jackson, MS I was elected deacon and served on the finance committee. I was also the Junior High School boys Sunday school teacher and sang in the choir. It seemed the more I served, the more I could serve. Every job and additional service was accomplished from a wheelchair. God did not remove my disability; God gave me the ability to overcome.

Stone Two - THANKFULNESS

My second memorial stone is thankfulness. I thank God that I am still alive, still breathing and can see the sunrise and the sunset of another day. I could have so easily died in my car wreck, and many were astounded that I did not.

> "Oh, give thanks to the Lord for He is good! For his mercy endures forever."

1 Chron. 16:34 NKJV

"And whatever you do in word or deed, do all in the name of the Lord Jesus, giving thanks to God the Father through Him." Col. 3:17 NKJV

"And let the peace of God rule in your hearts, to which also you were called in one body; and be thankful." Col. 3:15 NKJV

"Continue earnestly in prayer, being vigilant in it with thanksgiving."

Col. 4:2 NKJV

"Rejoice always, pray without ceasing, in everything give thanks; for this is the will of God in Christ Jesus for you." 1 Thess. 5:16-18 NKJV

"Be anxious for nothing, but in everything by prayer and supplication, with thanksgiving, let your requests be made known to God; and the peace of God, which surpasses all understanding, will guard your hearts and minds through Christ Jesus." Phil. 4:6-7 NKJV

"But thanks be to God, who gives us the victory through our Lord Jesus Christ." 1 Cor. 15:57 NKJV

And every creature which is in Heaven and on the earth and under the earth and such as are in the sea, and all that are in them, I heard saying, "Blessing and honor and glory and power be to Him who sits on the throne, and to the lamb, forever and ever!" Rev. 5:13 NKJV

Stone Three – FAITH

> Now faith is the substance of things hoped for, the evidence of things not seen. For by it the elders obtained a good testimony. By faith we understand that the worlds were framed by the word of God, so that the things which are seen were not made of things which are visible." Heb. 11:1-3 NKJV

> But without faith it is impossible to please Him, for he who comes to God must believe that He is, and that He is a rewarder of those who diligently seek Him." Heb. 11:6 NKJV

> For we walk by faith, not by sight. 2 Cor. 5:7 NKJV

My personal faith has grown and made surer by the little things in life. An example of this is finding a convenient parking space when the parking lot is completely full. This tiny answer has grown my faith by leaps and bounds because it happens over and over. God does use all things to increase my Faith for His glory.

I prayed that God would show Vienna her destiny, not mine. God answered in a way I never expected. I had the faith to accept this because God had built my faith on a thousand smaller things, like an open parking space in a full lot.

Stone Four – HELP

God's help. I have sought God and he has heard my plea. God has personally shown me how to do many things, some large, some small. Simple things like praying for an idea on how to make a repair on my motorcycle. God has either inspired an answer or directed me to a YouTube video. God gets the credit, every time. I know who my source is. God showing me in dreams ways to complete my home-made Volkswagen trike is another example of God's help, and it increased my faith greatly.

> "Call to Me, and I will answer you, and show you great and mighty things, which you do not know." Jer 33:3 NKJV

> "God is our refuge and strength, a very present help in trouble." Ps 46:1 NKJV

Stone Five – FULL ATTENTION

While going through the routine of life, I often overlooked the need for and importance of interacting with God. I know how to seek God and call for His help. God showed me that I need to be still and listen to him. How am I supposed to do that? I have found that God can and does use anything to get our attention. He has used the tragic and the mundane. He has used the loss of a job, the loss of a loved one, a missed business appointment, a divorce, an inconvenient red light. God wants my attention just like He wants yours. It is so simple. Be still and listen.

"He who has ears to hear, let him hear!" Matt. 15:11 NKJV

"Be still, and know that I am God. I will be exalted among the nations, I will be exalted in the earth!" Ps 46:10 NKJV

Stone Six – ANOTHER TOUCH FROM GOD

When I lost my legs, I was totally living for myself. I was living how I wanted without thinking much of what God thought about what I was doing. I was jogging, bicycling, hiking, SCUBA diving and I partied with pretty women. I was an athlete in great shape physically, but not spiritually.

After losing my legs, all I could see was everything I couldn't do. Everything I loved to do required physical movement, including the job I had. If I had the choice, I would have died rather than gone on as half of a man. The years of fancy prosthetics and accommodations for the physically handicapped were years away. Most of them I would never be able to use anyway because my brain injury limited my sense of balance. The world kept on moving, but my life stopped. I was overwhelmed with doubt.

And yet, God encouraged me through other people, through an inspirational book, through the everyday responsibilities, I was forced to get up and move regardless of how I felt. There came a day when God touched me to my very core, and I felt His presence. I experienced the runner's high after pushing myself past the end of my own endurance. I felt exactly like I had just finished a run. How could this be? My running days ended the day of my car crash. The use of my arms replaced my legs for movement in my wheelchair. God flooded my body with endorphins. I experienced the direct touch of God and His restorative powers. Suddenly, like the flip of a switch, I was no longer half a man. I believed I would never experience such healing. Tears of joy and thankfulness flowed. This was an unexpected gift from God!

> "But I discipline my body and bring it into subjection, lest, when I have preached to others, I myself should become disqualified." 1 Cor. 9:27 NKJV

> "Fear not, for I am with you; be not dismayed, for I am your God; I will strengthen you, I will help you, I will uphold you with my righteous right hand." Isa. 41:10 NKJV

> "I can do all things through Christ who strengthens me." Phil. 4:13 NKJV

> Therefore, do not worry about tomorrow, for tomorrow will worry about its own things. Sufficient for the day is its own trouble. Matt 6:34 NKJV

"And we know that all things work together for good to those who love God, to those who are the called according to his purpose." Rom 8:28 NKJV

"The Lord is on my side; I will not fear. What can man do to me?" Ps. 118:6 NKJV

Stone Seven – CHRISTIAN MOTORCYCLE ASSOCIATION

CMA returned the experience of "wind in my face." Jogging and running gave me wind-in-my-face joy. That joy was utterly lost the day I lost my legs. I love that feeling of total freedom of movement. It is like flying but flying without legs is surreal freedom. God has shown me that he cares about the tiniest joy He can bring to me.

My joys have included witnessing and serving God with a group of Christian believers. Riding in unison on the highway with each member and wearing the same Christian back patch is a witness that people see. My obviously altered motorcycle draws people to it like bees to a flower and people have questions. Everyone knows someone with a disability. This gives me a beautiful chance to witness about the glory and love of Jesus Christ. One thing encourages the other. God always wants me to witness. The joy of the wind in my face encourages me to ride and to witness every chance I can. It is a chance to change one heart at a time and I love it.

"For the Lord God will help me. Therefore, I will not be disgraced; therefore, I have set my face like a flint, and I know that I will not be ashamed." Isa. 50:7 NKJV

"Look at the birds of the air, for they neither sow nor reap nor gather unto barns; yet your heavenly Father feeds them. Are you not of more value that they?" Matt. 6:26 NKJV

"Delight yourself in the Lord, and He will give you the desires of your heart." Ps.37:4 NKJV

Stone Eight - GOD KNOWS MY THOUGHTS

God knows our every thought, good ones and bad ones, all of them. He knows the desires of our hearts and will reveal Himself to us and strengthen our faith, just like He does when He helps us find that ideal parking space.

I had just moved into a new apartment and my furnishings were sparse indeed. I needed a microwave oven, a recliner and I needed a copy of a government form. None of these things were big, but the oven and recliner were things I didn't have the money for at the time. I planned to save up and buy them, so I didn't tell anyone I was looking. But God knew.

Christmas was around the corner and my son came over one afternoon with a present for me. It was a good-sized present, but I was still surprised when it turned out to be a microwave oven. Nicholas was pleased that I was so happy.

A few days later a friend asked, "Could you use a recliner?" The recliner was nice, serviceable and I kept it for several years. I also took countless naps in it.

I can't remember the exact government form I was looking for, but I couldn't find it at the post office, the stationary supply store or the library. It happened so long ago that we didn't have a human resources manager. I decided to ask the secretary of the President of the company. It was a hectic day so I put off calling her. On a run to the copy room, I ran into said secretary. When I asked about the form I needed, she calmly took the top sheet of paper off of her pile and handed it to me. "Is this the form you're looking for?" It was exactly what I was looking for. Was it dumb luck? Chance? Happenstance? NO! Divine interventions. He knows our thoughts and our needs. Amen.

Trust in the Lord with all your heart and lean not on your own understanding. In all your ways acknowledge Him, and He shall direct your paths. Pro. 3:5-6 NKJV

> "And all things, whatever you ask in prayer, believing, you will receive." Matt 21:22 NKJV

> "But Jesus, knowing their thoughts, said, "Why do you think evil in your hearts?" Matt 9:4 NKJV (Jesus knows your bad thoughts, but also your good thoughts.)

Stone Nine - ANGER MANAGEMENT - GOD'S WAY

As I have said earlier in this book, my anger management skills were re-enacting the role model I had grown up with, "hit it, kick it, break it, cuss it." Even after I came to Christ, it was hard for me to react in any other way. But God showed me that after several failed marriages there was something wrong, and it was me. Without any condemnation from God, he showed me,

> "But the fruits of the Spirit are love, joy, peace, longsuffering, kindness, goodness, faithfulness, gentleness, self-control. Against such there is no law." Gal 5:22-23

I felt immediate remorse as God pointed out my many angry responses. I had been a Christian for years and was still acting in rage whenever something didn't go my way. I began to pray for God to remove this from me, and He has to a large extent. But, if I fall short anywhere, it is in this area. I am still a work in progress, but "Praise God, He loves me anyway!"

> "For I am persuaded that neither death nor life, nor angels nor principalities nor powers, no things present nor things to come, nor height nor depth, nor any other created thing, shall be able to separate us from the love of God which is in Christ Jesus our Lord." Rom 8:38-39

Stone Ten - SURRENDER THE FLESH

Another sin I have struggled with is pornography. It is only a click away on the internet or cell phone. Pop up ads will entice a man from every direction once that door has been opened. For me it had become an unstoppable cycle: sin then confess, sin then confess. I wanted to stop but could not muster the determination or strength to follow through. Conviction from the Holy Spirit became so heavy I could not bear the weight of it. Then God opened my eyes and my heart was ready to follow.

> "But I say to you that everyone who looks on a woman to lust for her has committed adultery with her already in his heart." Matt 5:28 NASB

> "Do you not know that the unrighteous will not inherit the kingdom of God? Do not be deceived. Neither fornicators, nor idolaters, nor adulterers, nor homosexuals, nor sodomites, nor thieves, nor covetous, nor drunkards, nor revilers, nor extortioners will inherit the kingdom of God." I Cor 6:9-10 NKJV

There it was, in the written word. If these things weren't out of my life, heaven would not be my eternal home. This had to stop! I had always thought of my pastime as fairly innocent compared to some of the things on this list. That wasn't how God looked at it, and this got my attention. I had to stop! But how? My answer was also found in God's Word:

> "Therefore submit to God. Resist the devil and he will flee from you." James 4:7 NKJV

Gradually, over a period of time, it became easier to resist. Like the "snowball" effect, the strength to resist grew. Successfully resisting actually became a joy. It became easier and easier to resist, until God took that desire completely away. No deep therapy needed - just Jesus. Don't misunderstand, this has nothing to do with controlling myself and everything to do with fully relying on God because I can't do it myself.

> "For we know that the law is spiritual, but I am carnal, sold under sin. For what I am doing, I do not understand. For what I will to do, that I do not practice; but what I hate, that I do." Rom 8:14-15 NKJV

Stone Eleven - FINANCES - GOD'S WAY

One of the final strongholds I struggled with was who was going to run my finances. I threw in money here and there as the collection bag was passed down the pews. I was nowhere close to a tithe and I wasn't faithful in what I did give. It was hit and miss, and in total disobedience with God's Word. I knew it, and yet, I would not trust God with my hard-earned money.

I justified my actions because I was living paycheck to paycheck. I was not a good money manager. I struggled with "pay bills" or "pay God" and that was the way I looked at it. It was an obligation I didn't want and never signed up for. But God showed me differently and sternly.

"Will a man rob God? Yet you have robbed me! But you say, 'In what way have we robbed You?' In tithes and offerings. You are cursed with a curse, for you have robbed Me, even this whole nation. Bring all the tithes into the storehouse, that there may be food in My house, and prove Me now in this," says the Lord of Hosts," Mal 3:8-10 (continued below)

I had read all of this before and it was the nut in the shell that fired my rebellion. For the first time, God made me continue reading and opened my eyes,

> "If I will not open for you the windows of heaven and pour out for you such blessing that there will not be room enough to receive it. Mal 3:10

> "And I will rebuke the devourer for your sakes, so that he will not destroy the fruit of your ground, nor shall the vine fail to bear fruit for you in the field," says the Lord of hosts. And all nations will call you blessed, for you will be a delightful land," says the Lord of Hosts. Mal 3:11-12

I started out skeptically at first, and then over the months, and now years, God has shown me the truth of tithing. I have all of my needs met and a great number of my wants. I am not rich by American standards. By world standards we are living at the top of the financial heap, just as God promised in Malachi.

Stone Twelve - A PEANUT BUTTER SANDWICH

I am not a picky eater and while I was still a working man, I would fix a sandwich for lunch and take it with me. Crunchy peanut butter with jelly was always a favorite, and still is for that matter. One Wednesday morning I was in a dither trying to fix lunch, take out the trash and gather my work uniforms for the laundry. I remembered I hadn't fed my golden lab. I quickly stuffed my uniforms in the truck, momentarily layed my PB&J sandwich on the rear bumper and pushed toward the house to feed Harley.

When I finally got settled in my truck and hit the ignition, I saw I would need gas before going anywhere. Great. I was in a sweat as I pulled out of the drive and headed to my favorite discount gas station two miles out of my way. There was so much traffic in front of the station I had to wait for a chance to turn left. When it finally came, I hit the gas to "shoot the gap," and hit the rain trough. My front end literally came off the ground and I bounced into the station.

The pump would not take my debit card. In those days I could still pump before I paid, but it was a pain in the neck to have to roll inside. I looked at the clock and realized that no matter what I did, I was going to be late to work. I hated to be late and now, traffic was worse than before. I was getting madder by the second.

And then I saw it. My PB&J sitting on the bumper of my truck where I had left it. After all the starts and stops and hitting the rain trough, lunch was not lost. I immediately calmed down.

God was with me in all my morning rush. It was time to appreciate my God who cared so much about me that even my sandwich was important to him.

> "Look at the birds of the air, for they neither sow nor reap nor gather into barns; yet your heavenly Father feeds them. Are you not of more value than they?" Matt 6:26 NKJV

Stone Thirteen - THE COCONUT JAR

"This jar started as a coconut," said the missionary from the Philippines, "And, it's not for sale." I was eyeing the unusually shaped jar. It was small, only about 4½" tall. It had a removable lid with a knob in the center for holding and the bottom was flat enough to keep the jar from toppling. What captivated me was the tiny, intricate painting of Philippino natives. They were holding hands and dancing in happy freedom around the diameter. I was fascinated by the jar and kept offering money until the missionary relented and sold it to me.

I was at a conference about an hour's drive from my home in Mississippi when I crossed paths with this Philippino missionary. He was the guest speaker. While I loved the jar I had purchased, it would be a few years before happy dancers would speak to me in a whole new language.

Sometime in the afternoon this missionary stopped me and explained. "On the way to the conference I had trouble with my car. I needed to have it fixed so I can get home." He continued,

"That repair cost exactly the price you paid this morning for my jar."

Our meeting was a divine appointment, that I thought was only for his benefit, but years later it turned out to be for my benefit, too. After I lost my legs, I would use this very jar to keep my tokens and remembrances (stones) for my altar. My tokens were small enough to fit and the happy dancers would eventually bring a smile to my face every time I looked at it.

> "And we know that all things work together for good to those who love God, to those who are the called according to his purpose." Rom 8:28 NKJV

Stone Fourteen – BUT GOD

Throughout the bible scripture begins with the same two words, BUT GOD. These are my two favorite words in the bible. How fitting that this would be one of my memorial stones. Have you had a "but God" moment or experience? Can you remember that time when you personally felt the presence of the Almighty? The following are examples in scripture where God has rescued, redeemed, and intervened to change circumstances for His glory.

Noah was the first rescue mission in Genesis 8:1 (NLT):

> "But God remembered Noah, and the wild animals and the livestock with him in the boat. He sent a wind to blow across the earth, and the floodwaters began to recede."

How many times has God had to throw out that life raft for you? I have lost track of the number of times our ABBA FATHER has helped me in His grace. Many years ago (1990's) I had a health issue. A visit to the urologist and an x-ray showed two black spots the size of quarters on one kidney. The word cancer was never mentioned, but an exploratory surgery was immediately scheduled. At a Wednesday night prayer meeting, I was anointed with oil and prayed over by the congregation. The next week after my surgery that same urologist reported to me that those two black spots could not be found! Hallelujah!

> "But God led the people around by the way of the wilderness toward the Red Sea. And the people of Israel went up out of the land of Egypt equipped for battle" Exodus 13:18 NLT.

The story of the children of Israel being led by the cloud of Jehovah God by day and a pillar of fire by night is an example of God's intimate relationship with us. It is amazing that the God of this universe and all creation would communicate one on one with everyone. Why not? We are His children. He hears our prayers and I know this because God answered my prayer when I prayed with the person in need on the telephone. The answer that I prayed for happened immediately. This humbled me and caused comfort, wonder and awe!

It was finished. Jesus had died on the cross and He was laid in a tomb.

> "But God raised Him from the dead" Acts 13:30 NKJV

It is never over until God has the final say! Praise God! God intervened in my life after my auto-accident that resulted in the amputation of both legs. I was in a coma for six-weeks. My family was told that I would be a vegetable, mentally brain-dead "if" I woke-up. But that did not happen!

These scriptures of "But God" vary by the translation and are only a portion of the actual references in the Bible. It has been my deepest desire to write only the words God has illuminated in my mind. I do not want to share a falsely fabricated story.

> "For I consider that the sufferings of this present time are not worthy to be compared with the glory which shall be revealed in us." Romans 8:18 NKJV

Paul pinned these words to the church in Rome and these words have become my perspective on life.

This manuscript has been a challenge to write. I have a hard time articulating the feelings and emotions of my journey with Christ. His power, mercy and grace continually overwhelm me. Knowing that my sins are forgiven, brings a peace and joy that continuously flows from within.

I was that person with no value, no purpose, no faith, and no hope. "But God" has changed all that disappointment, discouragement, failure, pain, and loss of my past. All my limitations, losses and longings are nothing when compared to Romans 8:18.

My prayer for you is to grow in Grace!

> "With men this is impossible, but with God all things are possible." Matt 19:26 NKJV

> "But seek first the kingdom of God and His righteousness, and all these things shall be added to you." Matt 6:33 NKJV

www.ingramcontent.com/pod-product-compliance
Lightning Source LLC
Chambersburg PA
CBHW072012110526
44592CB00012B/1275